ALSO BY ROBERT RANGEL

The Organ Grinder's Monkey
The Red Dot Club: Victims' Voices

The Red Dot Club

by

Robert Rangel

Copyright 2014 by Robert Rangel

Cover design by Christy Lifosjoe

More information at http://www.robertrangelbooks.com

ISBN: 978-0-9903173-5-7

The Red Dot Club / Robert Rangel

Dedication

This book is dedicated to all my fellow
Red Dot Club Members alive, and honored dead.
I salute you.

Red Dot Club Definition

This is a very exclusive club. It has very few members in relation to the population of the world. No one wants to be a member, and the mark of the red dot is forced upon those who after receiving it become members. This is the mark made on the human body after being shot.

—Taken from Robert Rangel's personal homemade dictionary.

Acknowledgements

To my academy Drill Instructor Ramrod, James "Jim" Mahone.

Feared by all, hated by some, loved by others.

Personally? I am and was of the latter group.

Thank you for making us bleed, throw up, and curse you. Your methods, harsh though they were, were correct.

I credit you with saving my life. Thank you.

—Robert Rangel
Los Angeles County Deputy Sheriff, Retired
Los Angeles County Sheriff's Academy, "The Hill."
Class 217

Contents

Introduction

Wyatt Earp and the O.K. Corral.

How many times have we heard the story, seen the movies? To my count there are eighteen movies and films on the O.K. Corral. Why? I'm not saying it's not a good story. It is. It is a true event which makes it all the better. But eighteen movies? Again I ask why?

I think it is because it titillates our imagination. What's it like to be in a gunfight? What were those guys like? Those guys must've been extremely tough, brave, smart, fast and the good was on their side, and they won. What a story.

But…you're missing something.

The here and now. They walk amongst us now. Real day Wyatt Earps.

Yep. I know, 'cause I know them. You might too and don't even know it. Some are my friends. Some are acquaintances. Maybe our real life, present Wyatt Earps are even braver and tougher than the original one. You decide.

Maybe the only difference between Wyatt Earp and these men is you don't know their stories.

Well, I'm going to tell you.

Ride Along

It was my first hour in a radio car. Ever. It was 1982, and I was a civilian. Not sworn. There was a program where if you had applied to be a Los Angeles County Deputy Sheriff Trainee you could go on a ride along.

The ride along program was instituted so you could ride in a radio car and see what it was like to work patrol as a deputy. It was an unspoken thing if you wanted to be a deputy, you should go on a ride along before getting hired.

Jerry was my cousin's husband. He worked at the Firestone Sheriff's Station. I knew so little at the time I did not realize the intensity of the crime that occurred in the Watts and surrounding area of Los Angeles. I later learned it was believed anyone who spent any time working patrol in the south area of Los Angeles could handle police work anywhere in the world. I came to believe it because when I later trained at Lennox Station, there were six murders in the first week where I worked in the Vermont area.

I was riding along with Jerry and his partner. A call went out. It was a man and woman fighting in the middle of the street. Other deputies had arrived before we got there and were breaking up the fight when we pulled up. The separated man and woman were quieting down as we got out of the car. Several other patrol units were standing by as backup to the handling unit. It was a balmy evening, about eleven thirty, and everything was quiet. The deputies were quietly talking to the couple and they were all polite saying, "yes sir" and "no sir" to the deputies. My heart slowed to a normal beat as I could see this call was a non-event.

Out of nowhere, it happened! Bam, bam, bamdamabam, bam, bam. Gunshots! Everyone suddenly looked at each other, and just as suddenly sprinted to their various radio cars, leaving the couple in the street looking after us. I realized this was for real. My heart was beating wildly, all my senses were on high alert, and my adrenaline was pumping. I was high. It was a weird mixture of excitement and apprehension. This was not some pretend movie; I was living it. We went to the end of the block and turned right.

An African American man was sprinting at us, wildly waving his arms in the air. He was hysterically yelling, "My cud'in, my cud'in, he done gone crazy!! I think he done kilt somebody!!"

We were going to the gunfire. Where the shooting was. I knew right then, there was nothing else I wanted to do than to be a Los Angeles County Deputy Sheriff.

—Robert Rangel

Follow Along

These stories include the actual locations where they occurred. The author has included the locations at the beginning of each chapter, so if the readers want, they can go to the Internet and look up the site and see the actual street view. In some instances, the places changed as the events unfolded. The street names are all included as they change so the reader can follow the route on their maps. In the chapter titled "Norco" at least one of the streets no longer continues through the route as told in the story. This is due to changing community developments, but for the most part the locations are still as they were and are very accurate.

Chapter 1

Induction into the Red Dot Club: Robert's Story

Hayworth Ave. and Norton Ave., West Hollywood, CA

I was sitting at the bar with Frank. I really like Frank. He is my kind of man. He has that sarcastic cop sense of humor I love. He is really smart. I love that too. He sees things when you don't think he sees them and is brave enough to say them as they really are. This is not popular with society nowadays. I don't care. I love that too. I'd rather sit with Frank and hear his blunt truthfulness than sit with a bunch of clueless tippy toe people.

Another thing I love about Frank is he can drink. That night at the bar he turned to me and said something I'd heard before but always discounted. When he said it I took notice, "You know you are a hero."

I looked at him, "No Frank. I just had that experience and survived."

He looked at me and said something else. That something else got me to thinking…

Humph. He got me thinking…

*****

Some months after the event, I was at Sean's wedding. It had not started yet. I was walking down the aisle of the church when a middle-aged woman came up and started kissing me on the cheeks. "Thank you, thank you." Kiss. "You saved him." Another kiss. "You saved my son." Kiss. "Without you he would be dead." Kiss, kiss, kiss.

I told her I didn't do anything. That it was nothing. She would not hear of it and denied me my protestations and continued to kiss me.

I write this now, thinking about her, and I get teary-eyed. I didn't tell her, but in the millisecond it happened I thought Sean would die. How can you possibly win a gunfight when someone has a gun to your partner's face? In that situation someone is going to die, and that someone that night was Sean because he was the one with the gun to his face.

But I'm getting ahead of the story.

*****

I was assigned to detectives at West Hollywood, but that night I was working overtime. It was a non-detective, nighttime, plainclothes assignment where we were going to find and arrest street-walking male prostitutes.

It was a simple operation. A plainclothes deputy in an unmarked car was to pick up a prostitute and make a deal. After the verbal deal was made, our deputy would give us a pre-arranged signal. He would stop the car and we would all swoop in and arrest the prostitute.

Getting ready for the operation, I was in the locker room with Paul. Both of us were always early for our shifts and were mostly alone in the locker room. As I got suited up, which that night consisted of a gun belt on blue jeans, t-shirt, bulletproof vest, and green raid jacket, I looked at Paul. Everyone called him Sweet Pea. He had the nickname before I met him because Paul was always happy and smiling. He was in a perpetual good mood.

But not that night. I looked at Paul and knew something was off. I asked him, "What's wrong?"

"I don't feel well," he answered.

"Shit Paul you look as sweet as ever," I smiled jokingly and said, "If you feel bad why don't you go home?"

"I'm not sick Bobby. I just don't feel good."

I was perplexed, "What do you mean? I don't get what you're saying."

"I don't get it either."

Now just to let you know I can be a bit of a pest when I want to understand something and I don't get an answer that satisfies me. "Paul, what are you talking about? If you feel bad go home, we have enough deputies to handle the operation."

"Bobby, I don't want to be here," he was obviously shaken, nervous. This was way out of character for him. "The last time I felt like this was before a shift in the sixties."

"What happened?"

"I came to work feeling bad. Just like tonight, I wasn't sick, but I felt really, and I mean really bad. I didn't want to be there. I suited up anyway and drove out in my radio car feeling really bad. It is impossible to describe. Midway through the shift I got a call of a man attacking people with an ax at the bus station. When I got to the bus station, there he was chasing and attacking people with an ax. He had chopped a few. He came at me with the ax and I shot him. Killed him. Afterwards, the bad feeling went away."

I looked at Paul, "Dude, I won't let anything happen to you. I love you Sweet Pea."

He looked at me and I could see my reassurances meant nothing to him. He still had that heavy doom overcast look hanging around him.

We all went to work.

After getting briefed and finding our rental cars, which were donated to us by the local rent-a-car agency, we hit the streets. My partner for the night was Sean. He was driving. Sean was fairly new to patrol. He had recently finished his patrol-training phase on the department and was just getting to be accepted and known as a trustworthy fellow deputy. All I knew about Sean was he had grown up in La Crescenta, a little community tucked away in the hills northeast of Los Angeles. It was known as "the rock" because the community is built on a dirt hill. But if you dig more than three inches down, all you find is rock, everywhere. The bastard was good looking. The girls loved him. He has a Martin Landau type of look, with those blue eyes and his face sprinkled with light freckles. Just to let you know ladies, he is much better looking than Martin Landau. He is half Mexican and half white, with a huge natural smile and huge white teeth that sparkle. Why couldn't I be half as good looking as him? He is the guy who when you are sitting in a bar laughing with three girls you just met, he walks in and the women melt into puddles and ooze over to him. Sean was in his mid-twenties. The bottom line is I didn't know Sean well and we were not friends. He was someone I had seen around the station and said hello to. But he had made it through the academy without quitting. Enough said, I trusted him.

I had been assigned to the station now for a little over five years, and as I mentioned before, I had just been assigned to detectives. The only reason I was working on this night was as a favor for another deputy named Dennis who had signed up for the overtime spot but had forgotten he had a trip planned with his wife to San Francisco. He begged me to take it. I did so to save his marriage; you know he had forgotten it was his anniversary (a lot of good that did, he ended up divorcing that wife anyway). Sean and Dennis were friends and had planned on working together that night until Dennis realized his stupid mistake no wife would understand.

I had grown up on the west side of Los Angeles near Westwood, two miles from U.C.L.A. Because of this people always assumed I was privileged and came from money. It's not true. My father put cans on shelves in a market for forty-three years doing what he loved. My mother decided she did not want to have someone else raise her children and worked part-time as a maid for the rich in Bel Air. We came from a lower middle-class income home, but we were happy. Both of my parents were born in the United States, and I grew up in an English-speaking household. I learned Spanish in school, and I speak it fairly well. I didn't do well in school but came out very close to the top in academics in my Sheriff's Academy class. It was like this, in high school I pulled a "B" in algebra for my first semester, and then I asked myself, "When will I ever use this?" I shut down and got out with a "D." Maybe someday I'll need that algebra, but not yet.

I am one of those tall Mexicans, six feet two and big, not fat, but big. I got tagged the name "Chief" in the Academy. One of my classmates said I looked like the big Indian in the movie *One Flew Over the Cuckoo's Nest*. I viewed myself as strong and fearless.

Sean and I found some male prostitutes at the corner of Norton Ave. and Hayworth Ave. We parked in the red zone on the northwest corner of the intersection facing south. A block west, at Norton Ave. and Laurel Ave. were Deputies Willie Robinson and Davis. Davis was driving a rented pickup truck, and Robinson was the passenger. Davis parked facing north.

It was midnight June 6, 1991. For you non-history buffs, that is D-Day, the day we invaded Normandy in 1944. It was an ominous date. It was a very, very dark intersection on a very dark night.

Sean and I were sitting in the car looking at all these male prostitutes. I'd just finished talking to a reserve deputy on the radio who was picking up or trying to pick up the male prostitutes. Just to let you know I am a pretty funny and sarcastic guy, and I had just finished making a funny and sarcastic remark to Sean, and he was laughing. We were both laughing.

In describing what happened next, I need to grope for the meaning for you. The word "suddenly" is too slow to describe what happened next.

"Immediately" is also a bit slow. "In the next instant" is closer but still not accurate. Ever trip and you can't stop it from happening? Ever been driving and look up, not realizing you had been looking down, to see the traffic was stopped? Like that. It was like that. What happened next was that fast.

I first saw the young man in front of our car. When I spotted him, he was between the right front headlight and the middle of the bumper, walking toward the left front headlight. He was looking at us through the windshield. I could not see either of his hands. They were together on the right side of his body. So if you are picturing this, the suspect (notice I went from young man to suspect) was walking in front of our car with both of his hands on his right side, shielded from our view. His upper torso was twisted away from us, but his head was twisted left and looking at us. What could he possibly be hiding?

He was walking really fast. Not strolling like normal people do when they cross the street; he was walking like he had a purpose. If he were to walk any faster he would be jogging.

I didn't see what was in his hands but when you put everything together what do you think was in his hands, a tootsie roll?

By the time I processed what was happening he was at the front left headlight. Maybe, and I mean maybe one second had now gone by. I said something to my partner, like what's with this guy. Honestly, I don't know what I said because things started to slow down really good by then. I knew I had to get my gun out of my holster. Like I had to get it out yesterday.

What you are about to read next is described over and over throughout the book so I may as well explain it to you now.

I'll explain stress. Yeah we all have stress. We feel stressed. That's not what I am talking about. I'm talking about an outpouring of adrenaline to your brain, heart, lungs, and muscles. Physiologically what that means is you think and process information faster than is humanly possible. You become stronger and faster than you ever thought possible. This is known as the flight or fight syndrome. Ever heard of it? Of course. Well I'm going to tell you about it for real. When adrenaline gets dumped into your system your brain goes into overdrive. This is so you can think your way out a situation faster than it is happening and you don't die. As your thought process speeds up, it is outpacing what is happening in real time. That means time... seems... to... slowwww...... dowwwwwn. Make sense? The Bible says we are wonderfully created, and I agree.

This was my third time since being on the job I was experiencing this phenomenon, and although I wasn't expecting it, I knew what was happening.

As I pulled my gun out of the holster, I extended my right arm over Sean's chest pointing my gun at the asshole (notice I changed to asshole now) who was slowly (at least in my world), turning to face Sean and who ended up in a two-handed frontal stance with his gun in Sean's face.

As I was thrusting my gun in front of Sean's chest, I flipped the safety off to shoot. It's just a little flick of the thumb and takes about as long as typing a letter on a computer keyboard. In my now slowed down surreal state, I could have counted off twenty seconds while my thumb did its job. Although I knew what was happening physiologically, I also knew there was not a millisecond to spare. I was mad at my thumb for not getting the safety off faster.

From the time I first saw the asshole to this point was no more than three or four seconds.

When I initially thrust my gun in front of Sean, he had not picked up there was a problem. He was still laughing. But in my world, there was nothing but getting my gun pointed at the suspect. To me things were happening in hours, but the reality was it was milliseconds. And as I pointed my gun over Sean's chest I saw him slowly follow my hand. I then saw him look to his left. Obviously he had seen the movement of the suspect. Somewhere in this time period, Sean had stopped laughing. When Sean turned his head left, he was facing this predator's gun. Point blank. Face to gun. It was a very nasty situation.

I had thoughts going through my head after the suspect got to Sean's door. I realized very calmly if we got out of the car, this criminal would realize we were cops by our telltale Sheriff's raid jackets and gun belts. He would shoot Sean who still had his gun in his holster. What choice did the suspect have? Although I had my gun out, I would not have been able to get out of the car and shoot and protect Sean. I knew either way, Sean was going to be shot, and possibly me too. I decided if Sean was going to be shot, I was going to make the suspect pay; I was going to shoot him hard!

Of course, this thought process took place within the time after the asshole turned and faced Sean and till the time it took him to get his gun in Sean's face. In real time it was just a millisecond, but it was a long time to me. Enough time to go through all the above thought processes.

Weighing options time was now over, I started shooting while Sean was face to face with the gun. Muzzle flash is exploding gunpowder, which is actual fire coming out of the barrel of the gun. If you look at it in real, non-adrenaline time the flash is just that. A very quick flash. Here and gone in the blink of an eye.

In my altered state, each muzzle flash, if I were to count them took a minute to complete. It was a slowly expanding ball of flame getting larger and larger. At its apex, the flame hung in the air, then slowly diminished to nothingness. Each bullet fired was a minute.

One bullet. Sean moved his upper torso to my lap, desperately twisting his face to the right as he did so, getting away from the gun in his face, (I guess he didn't want to see it coming).

When I shot, the suspect reacted almost simultaneously and shot back. But my first bullet was true and hit him in the lower abdomen. He shot just a millisecond after I hit him, but my bullet had done the trick. It had given us just a little edge, not much, but just a little wiggle room. My bullet buckled him a bit. This threw his aim off and he shot low and into the outside of the car's door handle. I shot again. And hit him again. He shot again. This time his bullet hit the outside of the door and went into the inner working of the window crank, which stopped the round. Honestly I didn't know if Sean had been hit when he went into my lap.

I shot him three more times, stitching him up his torso as he was going down. Each shot was taking about a minute to complete. Weird because my brain was wondering and yet understanding why each bullet was taking so long to get out. I was winning the fight that moments before I thought would be impossible to win. My body was slightly turned to my left but I was shooting sideways, that is with my right arm extended left over my body. I was not looking down my sights. Actually, I could not see my gun. It was that dark inside the car. But as I fired each round the muzzle flash illuminated my gun and I could see where my barrel was pointing. It was during these muzzle flashes, where I could see my gun that I made minute adjustments with my wrist, desperately trying to keep my gun barrel pointed at the suspect and stay on target. I was using the light from the exploding bullets to aim with.

I heard firecrackers behind me outside of the passenger car window.

I thought, *That's weird, why would anyone be lighting firecrackers right behind my head?*

A bullet slammed into me. From behind.

Fuck me, I thought, *I am so fucked. I'm getting shot from behind. How do I shoot both guys at once?*

I was ambushed. When the first bullet struck me it did so in the top back of my deltoid. The round entered the top of my shoulder and lodged itself in the top of my humerus. The upper arm bone, right in the joint.

This happened while I was shooting the suspect outside of the driver's door.

"Oh Robert," people often ask me, "Did you know you got shot when it happened?"

Oh yeah, I knew. Would you know if someone was trying to pull your arm out of its socket? Well that's what it felt like. Imagine someone pulling your arm out of its socket. I mean that's what it felt like after the feeling of getting hit by a baseball bat. Between that bullet and the second bullet I had many different, separate, although somewhat connected thoughts. *He's got me.* I thought, *there's nothing I can do. He'll aim a little higher and shoot me in the back of the head,* (in the ghetto this is known as getting shot in the back of the fo'head). I thought, *it won't be so bad. The first one went in really fast. I won't even feel a thing. It will be lights out. No biggie. Here it comes. I'm going to die.* What's weird is I should have been afraid. I wasn't. It was not fear, but acceptance of the situation as it was. I knew I couldn't win. I was trying to figure out how to shoot the guy at the driver's door, and at the same time shoot the guy behind me, and I was still physically shooting.

It was an impossible set of circumstances. I was focused on shooting the guy at the door. But at the same time if this makes sense, which it cannot, I was not focused because I was trying to figure out how to shoot the guy behind me. I was in serious pain, and furiously and desperately trying to figure out how to win. My mind was furiously trying to find a solution. I knew I was going to die. I thought Sean was possibly shot or dying or dead. I was out of options. I had nothing to lose. I was all of a sudden very, very sad. I wished my kids and wife, and mom and dad could understand I hadn't suffered when I got killed. I didn't want them to be sad. I just wished I could tell them it was okay, that it was not so bad, but I knew I wouldn't have the chance. That made me so sad. Then the second bullet hit me in my bulletproof vest, right at the lower part of my right scapula. When it struck me I thought, *fuck these guys.* I was still shooting, and the bullets hitting me were throwing my aim off, and I said to myself again with a little happy outlook, *Fuck these guys. I'm going to kill them both!* I knew I was going to die, but I was going to kill both of these guys anyway. I know it sounds weird, but I went from full acceptance of death, to deep sadness, to happy, like it was a little joke, to unbelievable outrage all in a millisecond. I was just beginning to fight, and I was ready to fight to the death. The word outrage is a complete understatement of what I felt. The word to describe how completely out of my mind angry I was has not yet been invented.

During all the mayhem my mind blanked out because I completely lost track of what was happening for a couple of milliseconds.

I didn't realize Sean was now out of my lap and had his gun drawn. I want everyone to understand how brave this was. Sean just had a gun to his face. He had just heard gunshots firing off at point-blank range but he still made a conscious decision to fight. To expose his head and fight. To come out of a place of relative safety and expose himself to mortal danger and fight was beyond brave. I use the word "brave" but I feel it is an understatement. I wish there was a better word for it. If you think I don't have the utmost respect for his decision you are sadly mistaken.

Bad news, the suspect at the driver's door was running. I couldn't believe it. Oh, I knew I had hit him, and numerous times too. How could he be running? I was having a dream, but it was real. It was a dream where you know it's just a dream and can't be happening, but it's happening anyway.

Good news. Sean was having none of it. The guy I had just stitched with bullets still had his gun in his hand. Real good news. The fact he still had a gun in his hand meant he was still a threat and was therefore very shootable. Sean had a perfect target. The suspect was running from the car in a straight-line perpendicular from Sean. Sean was banging bullets at him. I leaned over Sean's right ear and shot out of the window. Sean and I were both shooting at this piece of shit. He screamed and went down in the middle of the street.

I gotta tell you, my fucking arm, or I should say shoulder was scream-ing at me. The feeling of it being yanked out was intensifying.

As soon as Sean's suspect went down screaming, I screamed, **"NOW YOU, YOU SON OF A BITCH!!"** I heaved my chest up and out and thrust my upper body forward, thereby throwing my arm out of the passenger side window to shoot at the guy trying to kill me. This was the only way to get my gun on target. My arm wasn't working on its own. It needed the rest of my body to help it.

The coward was running. I took one shot at him. When I shot, he went forward stumbling. I thought I hit him, but I wasn't sure because he stumbled around the corner of a five-foot planter box and I lost sight of him.

Still out of my mind with rage I desperately searched for the door handle. I was going to chase this asshole who had tried to kill me! But I had a problem. When I went to reach for the door handle I couldn't find it. Things were now in normal speed. And I was blind. This has had happened to me before, (other shootings at night). Let me explain. Remember the muzzle flash? Let me ask you, what happens when it is pitch black and someone shines a light in your eyes and then turns it off?

You can't see, right? Maybe some red, blue or green spots every time you blink? I was literally blind. I was groping methodically feeling the inside of the passenger door panel to find the handle, and for the life of me I couldn't find it. Outraged like never before I wanted to catch the guy who shot me!!!

I sat there stupid as a dead rabbit. Blind as a dead horse. Impotent. Sean had left our car and was in the middle of the street. He was stand-ing over his now down, crying, hopefully dying, big brave man.

Sean ran back to our car. "I don't have my handcuffs." I gave him mine. He looked at me. "Are you alright?"

"No, I'm shot!"

He laughed hysterically and said, "I can't hear a fucking thing!" He ran off laughing back to the suspect to handcuff him.

I grabbed my radio to put out a call for help and I couldn't see as much as I felt the microphone push button. It was a walkie-talkie type radio with several different buttons and switches that changed to whom you were talking. I put out a request to have the air clear and that I had emergency traffic. "10-33." No response. I got no response. Our radio communication center should have come back with, "10-33 traffic go", or "10-33 traffic go ahead." That would have told me they had informed all units to shut up and I needed to broadcast. After what seemed like an eternity, one of the sergeants finally said, "Go ahead Bobby."

I then realized my hand-held radio was on a radio to radio frequency and not on a radio to Sheriff's Radio Control (SRC) frequency. So instead of telling the sergeant what had just happened, like I should have done, I fumbled with the radio and tried to figure out how to change the frequency so I could talk directly to SRC. That was a hassle. I couldn't see the numbers and letters on the radio. I was still blind. Finally I got on the right frequency, "10-33." I got my response, "10-33 traffic go ahead."

I was thinking stay calm when you speak so they can hear and understand you. "999, I've been shot. Norton... Norton... Norton," I pleaded. I had already fucked up the broadcast. I could not for the life of me remember the second street, Hayworth Ave. I just kept saying "Norton," the first street of the intersection I was on. The first thing you should do is tell SRC what station or unit you are. This tells them what station to focus their next broadcast to. This is so they're not sending a broadcast to a station 100 miles away to help you. The next thing you should tell them after your station is what unit you are. Then your location and what happened. What happened next is SRC asked me to identify myself. Of course. The problem is I didn't know who I was. This was an overtime spot remember? I had been assigned some funky unit identifier like 92FB1. It was not a normal unit identifier we used. They were all different unit numbers used just that night for that operation. I should have just said "West Hollywood." Then she would have known what station to send the information out to. I got my In-Service roster out. This is a list of all the units on duty on that shift. I started looking at the paper to see who I was. But I couldn't see the paper. I was still blind. I was really worried about where the bullet went. So here I was sitting in the car, trying to broadcast, fumbling with the buttons on the radio, talking to SRC, she was talking to me, asking me to identify myself. I was trying to read the paper, blinking furiously in the dark with these spots in my eyes. I still had my gun in my hand with the hammer back ready to shoot if the second suspect came back. She finally explained it to me, "I need you to identify yourself." At the same time I finally read the paper and did it right, "West Hollywood 92FB1, I've been capped, Norton and Hayworth Ave. Give me the patch." I finished up the broadcast giving a description and last seen direction of the shooter.

I started wondering if I was bleeding to death, or if the bullet went through any major arteries or my heart. Those thoughts scared the shit out of me, and I shoved them out of my mind. I decided to feel good about the pain I had, as it was isolated to my shoulder and back. I sang to myself, "Boy, that was close…the bad man almost got me," and I laughed.

I finally got the door open and got out of the car.

Deputy Robinson ran up. Remember he had been a block away with Davis? Robinson looked at me, "Bobby. What the hell happened? I heard the shooting!"

"I'm shot Will," I said. I was reassured by Robinson's presence. Former Marine. Six feet three inches of pure muscle, sinew and kindness with 22-inch arms.

"Where the hell is Jimmy (Davis)?" I asked.

I was still a little high on adrenaline and was kind of pacing around.

It turned out Robinson, who was running on the south side of the street eastbound to help me, passed the guy who shot me, while he was running west on the north side of the street. God help the bastard had Robinson gotten a hold of him.

It seemed Davis, in his attempts to turn his rental car around to get to me to help me, crashed into a few parked cars. Robinson finally had enough of it and just sprinted over.

Robinson said, "Sit down Bobby," and pointed to an abandoned sofa sitting on its side in the front yard of an apartment building. He said, "You're okay, remember you're the big Indian who can," and smiled that smile of his everyone loves. He put me at ease. "Does it hurt?"

"Yeah, Will, it does."

By now helicopters, Sheriff's cars, fire engines and paramedics were on scene. They hooked me up to some saline solution and asked me to hold the bag. So, there I sat with my shirt tucked in my jeans, but it was cut to ribbons and hanging down around my waist like some hula dress. I was topless, sitting on an upended discarded sofa and holding the saline solution bag connected to me with a needle. Deputies, my friends, kept coming over to me. They looked at me and then looked at my Red Dots. Then they looked at me again, "Bobby, does it hurt?"

"Yeah, it hurts a lot. Why?"

"Because you're just sitting there holding the bag, like nothing is wrong."

"No, it hurts."

"Oh."

This happened about three times, very weird. The same looks, the same questions, my same responses. The fourth time, I kind'a lost it, "Yeah it fucking hurts, man. What do you think?" I was smiling though when I said it; I was only half serious. I walked into the ambulance when they were ready for me.

The man who had put a gun to Sean's face was lying in the middle of the street screaming, moaning and whimpering. At times he was crying, especially when the paramedics were moving him around cutting his clothes off to work on him to save his life. I guess it hurt.

If I sound callous you bet I am.

It turns out the evil scum lying in the street was a gang member. He had been out of prison two weeks at the time Sean, and I met him. Why had he been in prison? For robbery. Robbery is defined as the taking of another person's property from them by means of force or fear. Guess what the subsequent investigation showed? That he and the guy who shot me wanted to steal our car, oh sorry, rob us of our car so they could use it in a drive-by shooting on a neighboring gang. See if they took our car, and if anyone got the license plate, it would show up as stolen and could not be traced back to them. It seems they had a car a block away with AK 47s to use in the drive-by.

*****

It must have been a busy Saturday evening. They couldn't come up with two ambulances. The sergeants at the scene were worried the suspect might die. What would the press say if they let a poor downtrodden man die in the street after some bloodthirsty deputy shot him? Then again they couldn't be sure I might not be bleeding out.

They had to make a decision and they did. Send them both in the same ambulance. So they sent the suspect and me in the same one. He was lying on a gurney in the back with Sweat Pea watching him, and I was sitting in the front seat. An ambulance attendant and a Los Angeles County Fire Paramedic were also in the rear of the ambulance with the suspect.

On the ride over we would hit little bumps in the road. The suspect would groan. I was so enraged I started yelling at him, "DIE MOTH-ERFUCKER!!! YOU'RE DYING. DOES IT HURT?! GOOD! I HOPE IT HURTS! YOU KNOW YOU'RE DYING!!! FUCKING DIE!!!" This went on two or three times. It was a good thing I didn't have a gun on me or I'm sure I would have killed him. The ambulance driver, Sweat Pea, the paramedic, and the ambulance attendant were completely quiet when I went on the tirades. They looked panicked as to what I would do.

As I was lying in the hospital bed, Paul came up to me with a huge smile. Just like the Sweet Pea I knew. "Hey, Bobby. I told you I had a bad feeling. Hahaha," He was standing over me laughing, "But it's gone now. Everything is okay." And off he went chuckling.

I got shot and everything was okay?

Later, Dennis wrote on my get-well card, "Thanks for taking my over-time 'SHOT!!'"

Fucking cops. You gotta love 'em.

I spent about three hours in the hospital. They x-rayed my shoulder. My doctor, (the same doctor who had previously fixed my knee), gave me a hug and said, "God loves you."

"Why?" I asked.

"Because the bullet burrowed in your upper arm bone, your humerus. Robert no bones shattered. It missed your scapula. I just can't believe it. Nothing is broken or shattered. Do you understand God really loves you?" He couldn't believe it. He said only God could have put the bullet in my shoulder where it was and not damage my arm and shoulder. As he was walking away, I heard him tell a nurse, "That guy is a real hero."

I got a little Band-Aid on my red dot and went home. I took an aspirin and went to bed.

*****

Several months later I was sitting at my desk in detectives. It was somewhat common the firefighters would come through the station. I looked up from my desk and there stood a six-foot-five firefighter. I smiled and said hello. He smiled back and said hello. I went back to work. I wrote a little on a report and noticed he didn't move. He was just standing there. I looked up again and he asked me, "You don't remember me do you?"

"No," I answered.

"You don't remember that night?"

"What night?"

"I was there."

"Where?" I asked.

"The night you got shot."

I looked him in the eye. "Were you in the ambulance?"

He nodded his head yes.

I smiled.

He spoke, "You were pretty angry."

Now I nodded my head yes.

"If you could have you would have killed him, wouldn't you?"

Again I nodded my head yes.

"Are you okay?"

I was scheduled to have surgery to have the doctor look inside my shoulder to see what the bullet was doing to the joint. It felt like it was scraping around the cartilage. I answered, "I'm good."

He said, "Cool" and left.

*****

I want to vomit when I hear the news calling some sports figure a hero. I want to vomit when our citizens place and honor these sports figures above those who truly make a difference day after day and night after night. Why are they called heroes? Because they put a ball in a hoop? Or put a ball in a hole in the ground? Or because they outran everybody else? What a bunch of shit. They cheapen the word and devalue the meaning of who heroes really are. I know so many who willingly go into a house where they know a man with a gun is waiting for them. Risking everything. Real life danger, not pre-planned scenarios where someone accomplishes some feat, but live and active scenarios where lives are lost.

I don't and didn't consider myself a hero. A hero, in my opinion is someone who purposely makes a decision to risk it all knowing he could die. I made a decision to fight and I had resigned myself to the fact Sean would die and I couldn't save him. I knew we couldn't get out of the car. I had no other choice but to do what I did and I made a decision there would be violent consequences to those who brought war to us. And it was done decisively, desperately, and with all possible extreme violence. We both survived. You think we were just lucky? No. Our actions that night saved our lives, and we acted bravely, without flinching against overwhelming and impossible odds, both of us. But it doesn't make us heroes. We were thrust into a situation against our will and won.

I am glad though if there was someone who was going to get robbed that night, it was us. I often think of the unprotected citizens who these animals prey on. Wives, children, innocent people who have done no wrong. The little six-year-old girl riding her bicycle who gets shot a half-mile away from a just occurred drive-by shooting. A little boy of three sitting on his porch with his parents and getting shot playing with his G.I. Joe action figure. You think I speak from fantasies or stories I've read in the newspaper? No, I speak from experience. It is not some far removed fantasy. These occurrences hurt me more than me being made a member of the Red Dot Club. I chose to put myself in harm's way. It was the life I chose. The innocents do not.

We saved someone else from being victimized that night and who knows who else in the future. I am very, very proud of that.

I loved it when Sean asked me if I was okay, and then laughed hysterically when I told him I was shot. He couldn't hear me because I had shot right next to his left ear as he turned away from the convict, and then again over his right ear when he was shooting out of the window. Both ears blasted. When he laughed, it was like he was laughing at death and standing up to it and saying, "Fuck you!!"

*****

It's like I told Frank, I had the experience and survived. But Frank made another statement that night in the bar I didn't tell you. It's the one that got me to thinking. "Bobby," he said, "You and I know that many could not have done what you did."

Would others have done the same? Would or could Wyatt Earp have?

*****

If the media had really done a story on this piece, the guy who put a gun to Sean's face would have been depicted as a 12-year-old boy on a bicycle. The media would have asked how two deputies could have shot him, a nice young man, a football star who tutored kids.

He got 14 years to life for his second convicted felony, this time using a gun. That meant he had to do 14 years before he could even be considered for parole.

He was out in seven.

I shot seven times, Sean shot six. The convict shot two times, (I think he would've shot more but he was busy trying to figure out what went wrong, why it hurt, and how to get away). I took two bullets from behind. I'm not sure how many shots the guy behind me fired, it sounded like five or six. But at a minimum it was the two that hit me. That's at least a total of seventeen bullets, maybe more. The gunfight lasted, according to Robinson, from the first shot to the last, no more than five seconds.

*****

The guy who shot me got away, never to be seen again. Oh I'm sorry he was seen again. You see we could have caught him. But we didn't. When he ran, he only went one block west to Laurel Ave. He hid behind an apartment complex trash dumpster. Our dog search, (K-9), started searching too far away. By the time the dog got to Laurel Ave., the dog was too exhausted to continue.

But that's not why we didn't catch the guy. We still could have caught him. I just told you we saw him again. I'm sorry it wasn't us, it was a neighbor. A neighbor saw all the police activity and looked out of his window to see what all the excitement was about. When he looked out, he saw the guy hiding behind the trash dumpsters. After the deputies left, several hours later, the suspect just got up and walked away. He saw that too. The neighbor called the station the next day and told the deputy that he had seen a short male Hispanic hiding behind the dumpster.

I don't care. The courts would've just let him out in a couple of years anyway.

Chapter 2

Off Duty

Pepper Brook Way and Azusa Blvd. Hacienda Heights, CA

I was at one of my favorite lunch restaurants, with one of my favorite people, eating my favorite dish.

Frank was talking. "Bobby, did you get the Medal of Valor for what you did?"

"No."

He was staggered, "Damn, you saved your partner's life, and then you shot the guy with the gun to your partner's head. You got shot, then you spun around to shoot it out with the guy who shot you. That's Medal of Valor stuff. What are you supposed to do to get the Medal of Valor?"

I shook my head, "There were five or six other shootings our department got involved with right after mine that got bad press. I think the department wanted to just get away from any press whatsoever about shootings."

He stared at me. He was incredulous, "But yours was a good shooting!" He shook his head again as if to say, "What a shame."

I was quietly eating. After a while he started talking. When he got to the part about the blood on his hands and that his one-year-old boy had just been killed I stopped eating. My stomach was in knots and I wanted to cry.

*****

I met Frank throughout my life, here and there. I'd see him about every six years or so. Shortly after getting the job where I currently work I walked down the hallway and there he was. He was talking to a couple of other cops. I stopped and looked at him and said, "Hi Frank." I could see his mind reaching for my identity. He knew he knew me, but from where he couldn't figure out. He forgot his cousin. It's not unusual in Mexican families. Sometimes I think we are lucky we didn't meet a girl at a party and after kissing her a bit find out later she's related.

Frank is about five years younger than me. My grandfather, Candelario Rangel, was born to Cruz Rangel in 1903 in El Paso, Texas. His mother died when he was ten. Cruz remarried and they bore a child, Manuel Rangel. My grandfather was fourteen years old when Manuel Rangel was born. Manuel Rangel is Frank's grandfather, my grandfather's half-brother. Manuel Rangel is over ninety-five years old now. He works outside every day on his ranch. He eats the food he raises. He believes in God, hard work, and family. He believes in right and wrong. In today's world he is considered old-fashioned with old-fashioned values, with no understanding of what the world and its morals are about. They are wrong, he understands. That's why he holds on to the old values. He raised all six of his daughters with the same values. Those values have been instilled in Frank.

So, throughout my life I had seen Frank at various family weddings and funerals and such. I knew he was a Los Angeles Police Officer, but as so many cops think, "If I didn't work with you I really don't know you," he and I were not particularly close. In fact, he knew so little about me that I found out later he thought I was a Santa Monica Police Officer.

Over the course of the next seven years, Frank and I occasionally lunched together. Sniffed each other out, like two dogs to see if we liked each other. It turns out he and I agree on pretty much everything. We've seen the same horrors.

*****

Frank is a really good-looking man (why do I have to be the ugly one?). He was well known in his neighborhood as a jock.

He is very muscular, with huge biceps. Like his grandfather, he loves God, his family and traditional values.

After competing as a collegiate athlete, Frank joined the Los Angeles Police Department in November 1987.

At the time the Los Angeles Police Department had a six-month academy. Thereafter there was a one-year patrol training probation period.

In September 1988 Frank was in the middle of his probationary period. He was doing well and expected to pass. At the time he was working the Central Patrol Station, which covered downtown Los Angeles. Downtown is a mixture of old and new businesses, in old and new buildings. Minutes apart from each other are homeless people, business people, drug dealers, secretaries, and civil service employees. Some buildings are seventy-years old, others are new. It contains a complete mix of races and food, and is not lacking for action.

Frank's training officer liked making drug arrests, and on September 21, 1988, Frank and his training officer were in court testifying on one of the arrests they had made. They had arrested a gang member they had observed selling crack. At the time he was arrested he was in possession of close to five hundred rocks of crack. That is a good arrest.

"Bobby, he was held to answer."

Folks, that means the court found there was sufficient evidence to proceed with the charges and to try him in superior court.

"Right after he was held to answer and as my training officer and I were leaving the courtroom, a guy in the courtroom looked at us and made the sign of a gun with his hand."

Frank then made the sign, with his index finger pointed out, his thumb up, and his three remaining fingers clenched to his palm, simulating a gun.

"Bobby, as he stared at us he put his hand to his head and made the motion of shooting himself in the head. When we got in the hallway, I told my partner we just got threatened. We pulled him out of the courtroom, into the hallway. He said, 'You're dead motherfucker!' We hung onto him and called the station. When a unit arrived, we arrested him for threatening a police officer."

"Who was he?"

"Some gang member. I guess he was a friend with the guy we just testified against. I mean he made the threat right after the guy was held to answer. It was my day off. I was sick with the flu; I had a fever and just felt like crap. It was now about one p.m. My mother was watching my little guy."

Frank affectionately called his young boy, "my little guy."

"I had a brand new red Toyota truck. It had a bench seat. It was a three-seater. My little guy was one and a half years old. Still in diapers. He was my world. The reason I worked. The reason I lived. I was so sick, and after court, my fever was rising, getting worse; it was high. All I wanted to do was go to my mom's house, pick up my little guy and go home. When I got to my mom's house, she saw how I looked. She made me some soup. She told me, 'Go to sleep. I don't want you to go home Frank. You're sick. Call your wife. Stay here for the night and get some sleep and rest.' I fell asleep on the couch. I slept until 9:30 that night. When I woke up, again my mom told me to call my wife and stay the night. But I wanted to go home. I got my little guy and put him in the car seat in the truck.

"Yeah. I remember my windows were fogged. My rear window was so fogged I couldn't see out of the back. As I was driving east on Pepper Brook Way about three blocks from Azusa, a car behind me started flashing his lights. I slowed. I pulled to the right to let them pass. I was so sick, I was just trying to get home. They could have passed me, but all of a sudden they drove right up to my bumper at a really high rate of speed. Just before I was sure he was going to hit me because he didn't have enough time to stop, he slammed on his brakes. My rear window was fogged and I couldn't see the car, just the headlights. I was alarmed and sped up. The other car then slowed and allowed some distance between the rear of my car and the front of their car. Then he did it again. He sped up and almost hit me, rear-ended me. This went on for several blocks, about three times. I was really on edge by this time. What the hell was going on? The hair on the back of my neck was standing up. I blew through a stop sign trying to get away from the car. I was angry, nervous, but still in control. At eastbound Pepper Brook Way at Azusa, there is a traffic light. There are two lanes there, a left lane where you can go straight into the Puente Hills Mall, or turn left onto northbound Azusa Ave. There is a lane to the right where you can turn southbound onto Azusa or go straight into the Puente Hills Mall. I was in the left lane. There were two cars in front of me. We were all stopped at the light. There was an open lane to my right. The car then pulled in to the empty lane to my right. He turned his car left so his driver's window was facing the front of my truck, but off to the side of his lane. It was a small car, like a Datsun B210. He was about thirty feet in front of me. Bobby, there were three guys in the car going completely ape shit!"

"What do you mean?"

"All three were jumping around in the car. Yelling, screaming, pointing their arms and hands at me. I thought, 'What the hell is going on?' Then it happened. As clear as your face is to me right now I can still see the passenger leaning down. He pulled up a rifle and aimed it at me. I saw it. It had a scope on it. I had a brand-new truck. There weren't even any plates on it yet. They were going to carjack me. My training kicked in. My training from the academy. They were slightly in front of me.

I went to back up so I could put my engine block between them and myself. After I did that, I could face them head-on. I fully intended to shoot it out with them."

"What gun were you carrying?"

"I had a five-shot 38 caliber Smith and Wesson in my holster on my right hip. When I went to put the car in reverse, I ground the gears."

"You had a stick shift?"

"Yeah. When I ground the gears, it snapped me out of taking action. My little guy was in the car with me. In the Academy, in officer survival training, one of the incidents they told us about was the Los Angeles County Sheriff's Deputy who walked in on a store robbery. He had his kid with him. He engaged the robbers, and the kid was killed."

I remembered the incident. I also learned about the incident when I went through the Academy. A reserve deputy was going to the market with his kid. I think the child was under five years old. As he was approaching the market, he saw either one or two guys in the store with guns robbing the place. He retreated and got down behind the tire of his car in the parking lot. When the robbers came out of the store gunfire was exchanged. A bullet skipped off the ground and killed his child.

"Bobby, I wept when I heard that story. It broke my heart. The kid dying. Just horrifying. The grinding of the gears, I don't know why, but it made me remember this gut-wrenching story. After not being able to get in reverse I sped around to the left of the cars that were stopped in front of me. I blew the red light and went north on Azusa. I got on the 60 freeway, west, away from my home. I didn't want them to know or have any idea where I might live. That was really hard."

"What was Frank?"

"Putting my tail between my legs and driving away. I was running like a coward. I hated it. It bothered me. It went against my grain to run. When I looked in my rearview window, I could see the car getting on the onramp following me. It was making the curve on two wheels. Then I remembered. The threat. Court. The guy who threatened to kill me earlier that day. They are going to kill me. By now I had put my gun between my legs because I didn't have time to holster it. I quickly got the truck up to 100 miles an hour. I was honking my horn, flashing my lights, changing lanes going around cars. I drove in the emergency lane, and then quickly passed to the number one lane, back and forth, zigzagging through traffic. Crazy, desperate driving, barely in control, never slowing down below 100 miles an hour. I was passing cars like they were standing still. Every time I looked in the mirror, they were following me. I thought, 'If they shoot the tires my little guy and I are dead. The truck will flip, and we'll die. Someone will hopefully call the CHP. I'll run into a cop on the freeway. Someone is going to call the cops, they have to, this is too crazy.' In those days there were no cell phones. This was in the eighties. I was hoping someone would stop and call the cops."

As Frank was telling the story, my heart was pounding.

"Bobby, traffic slowed in front of me. I had nowhere to go. I couldn't go around any more cars. I hit the brakes."

"Where were you Frank?"

"I was near the Indiana off-ramp, still on the 60 freeway."

I googled it. Frank had covered 18 miles. How many people have driven 18 miles, at over 100 miles an hour, weaving in and out of traffic and in the emergency lane without crashing?

"I was now in the fast lane, the number one lane. The car was behind me. My little guy had been crying non-stop for some minutes now. I reached over and grabbed the seatbelt, which was holding my son in his seat and just ripped. I tore it off. I tore the seatbelt clasp open with my bare hand breaking the seatbelt open. Things slowed down then.

Everything was in slow motion. The car behind me fired through the rear window. I was pulling my son... my life, out of his seat, desperately pulling him to me, cradling him under my right arm to protect him. Simultaneously a bullet smashed into the rear window. When the round came in it blew shards of glass through my scalp and into the back of my head. The impact of the bullet was so fierce it blew the glass violently into my skull, embedding itself into the bone. Instantaneously I had an awful, deep fire-like burning in my skull. A second bullet tore through the rear window. It missed me. These were all separate and distinct events. Each one was a long agonizing ordeal to be endured. But the reality was they were occurring within milliseconds of each other and almost together at the same time. When the second bullet came through the passenger cab, it seemed to slowly and lazily whiz around. I could hear it. It was like an angry pissed off bee. I could hear it screaming and buzzing, searching to kill. 'Please dear God, not my son,' I prayed. I was covering his head with my right arm, and as much of his body as I could. I was thinking I needed to keep any of the bullets from hitting him. It didn't matter how many times I was shot as long as I could save him. The car was coming up on my right side, forcing another car to my right over to its right."

Frank was showing me with his hands the positions of the cars.

"They had now pulled beside me. They continued to fire through the passenger window and door. I could see the dust of the glass, as the bullets passed through the window. Cars were now aware of the shooting. They were screeching, braking, speeding up, and crashing into each other. Smoke was everywhere. It was total mayhem. There was metal all over the freeway, there was glass all over the interior of my car. Multiple bullets were now whizzing in the cab. Bobby, I was still driving really fast. I was crouched down low. So low I couldn't see out of the front windshield. I don't know who drove my truck. It wasn't me. I don't remember driving. I still don't know who drove my truck. To this day, I wonder how I never crashed. But I know I wasn't driving. I felt so helpless."

I looked at Frank. He looked at me like he was asking me who was driving his truck. I had no answer for him. "Bobby, I don't know who drove my truck for a while. It wasn't me.

"I felt a thud on the side of my right arm. I knew I had just been shot, but I felt no pain. I don't know why except maybe it was adrenaline or because the burning in my head was so overpoweringly more painful. I got shot right in the spot of my arm that was covering my little guy's head. He was under my armpit with my arm draped over his head and as much of his body as I could cover. Again I prayed, 'Dear God, please don't let the bullet pass through my arm. Please let all the bullets stay in my body and not pass through me into him.' I was doing everything I could to protect my son. Another thought, 'If anyone is going to die, please let it be me.' I accepted death as an acceptable alternative to my son dying. Then the thought came to me, 'If I die, my son dies. If I crash, my son dies. If I'm shot and die, my son dies.' The bullets were lazily whizzing around in the cab of my truck like a bunch of buzz saws. Time was so slow. They weren't stopping. By now they had fired eight times. We were driving side by side, and they were still firing. My baby had stopped crying now. I looked at my hand. The hand belonging to the arm cradling my son was covered in blood. I knew it wasn't my blood. My son, the light of my life was motionless."

Frank looked at me, "Bobby, they killed my son. I just knew it, whereas he had been crying non-stop, he was now motionless with his eyes closed and not crying anymore. Limp. It wasn't my blood on my hand. I thought, 'THESE FUCKERS GOTTA DIE!' The guys were now pulling off the freeway. I reached down between my legs for my gun, and it was gone. During all the action my gun had fallen on the floor somewhere. I quickly groped around the floor with my left hand, but couldn't find it. I was shaking my son. Bobby, all this is happening in milliseconds. Slow motion, but in milliseconds. I was shaking him. 'If he dies, I have to kill them.' I decided I was going to take my truck and run them over, I was going to ram them until they crashed and then I was going to run them over. I was enraged, beyond enraged. I saw he was shot in the leg. For the third time I prayed, 'Please not the femoral artery, don't let his femur be shattered.' That's when he started crying."

As Frank was talking, I realized I had been holding my breath.

"I went from kill mode to save mode. I had to save my son. I drove to Central Division where I worked. A couple of my friends were on duty. They scooped us up and drove my son and I code three to White Memorial Hospital. I rushed my son inside. The doctors assured me my son was going to be all right. After I discovered my son was going to be okay, I checked myself out of the hospital. I had glass in my skull, and it was burning. I'd been shot in the arm. I had a high fever. I looked at my partners, they looked at me. I said, 'Let's go get them.'

"As I was walking out to get in a radio car to get the guys, the lieutenant, who had also responded to the hospital asked me, 'Where are *you* going?'

"I said, 'To get the guys who shot my boy.'

"The lieutenant said, 'Get your motherfucking ass back in the hospital!'

"I did as I was ordered."

"How were you going to get them Frank?"

"Bobby, when they pulled in front of me on Pepper Brook I got a good look at them and their car. We were going back to the area where it started to look for the car."

I was incredulous that he was ready to go battle with a fresh bullet in his arm, glass embedded in his skull and running a high fever.

"Bobby, for years and years, it bothered me I'd ran."

"Jesus, Frank, you had your baby with you. I'd a done the same thing."

"It still bothered me."

*****

"The Los Angeles County Sheriff's Department handled the investigation. Two Industry Station detectives had the case. They actually played good cop, bad cop with me. They didn't believe my story. One of them kept insisting I had done something to instigate the incident. During their interview with me, I got so pissed off I told the 'bad cop' if he didn't leave I was going to kick his ass.' He left the room and I didn't see him again."

*****

"The cops, my partners, guarded us. They guarded my son. The outpouring of concern shown to my family was truly heart touching. After my son got out of the hospital we went into hiding. My little guy was walking around normally on one leg and on his tippy toe with the other leg. My wife was angry because she was thinking, as I was, I was shot because of my testimony earlier in the day of the shooting. I told her if we found out it was job-related, I would quit and find other work."

*****

"After the shooting while I was at the hospital, the driver and his two companions went to a party. Attending the party was the little brother of my best friend. He had been my best friend since I was nine years old. The driver told my best friend's little brother, who was a doper, he had just shot someone in a new red Toyota pickup truck. The next day the news of the shooting was everywhere, in the media, and especially in the neighborhood. Everyone knew me. My best friend's little brother told my best friend who had shot me. My best friend told his little brother to not tell anyone. He said if the Sheriff didn't figure it out in a week, they would disclose the information."

"Frank, your best friend hid the information?"

"Yeah, my best friend."

"Of course, secrets like that get out. After four days my best friend was attending another party. He couldn't keep quiet any longer. He told a mutual friend of ours who the shooter was. My other friend asked my best friend, 'Are you nuts?' He immediately called the Sheriff's Department.

"The Sheriff's Special Enforcement Bureau (Los Angeles County Sheriff's equivalent of SWAT) came to the shooter's house. The shooter came out of the house with a rifle. The deputies did not shoot him. He was arrested.

"The driver it turns out had been smoking crack cocaine that day. He was a gang member that lived seven doors away from my mom. That's where the arrest was made. He had gone to school with my little sister."

Frank stopped talking. I stopped. After a while he continued. "Before the shooting, all three guys who were in the car had been at a house where one of them lived. They were smoking crack and ran out. They agreed to go and rob a drug dealer of their dope. Before they left, the driver, who was the supposed shooter showed the two others his 22-caliber rifle he had in his car. The guy whose house they were visiting had some 22-caliber bullets and gave them to the driver. When they left the house, they had the rifle and bullets. This incident, it turns out had nothing to do with the threat I had received earlier in the day at court. The driver decided he just wanted to 'fuck' with a guy who had a new truck. That's it. Such a little thing. This guy's got a new truck. Let's fuck with him.

"You know what really angers me to this day?"

"What is that Frank?"

"The deputies were happy. They were able to get the two passengers to place the whole blame of the shooting on the driver. This assured them an easy conviction or plea bargain. All three were guilty. The rear passenger provided the bullets. The front passenger is the guy who initially pointed the rifle at me. How in the hell could the driver have been shooting at me while driving on the freeway at 100 miles an hour? Yet this is what they both told the detectives, and the detectives believed them. The two passengers told the detectives they only wanted to go and get more crack, not to shoot anyone."

I shook my head. Having been a detective, sadly I agreed.

"If I had not gone through the Academy, I don't think I would have made it. I had the will to survive. I was able to drive and not crash although there was a time I didn't know who was driving the car. If I was a civilian, I don't think I would have survived.

"Bobby, the guy got twelve years. They convicted him of attempted murder on a police officer. He was nineteen years old at the time. He did two years at California Youth Authority, then transferred to an adult prison where he did another five years. He did seven years, just like the guy who tried to kill you."

Frank's face turned into an ugly scowl. "Our country, our society says life is precious. We don't act like it. We continuously let very bad people out. When are people going to understand how evil some people are? What's it going to take? We go out every day to try and catch these bad people, and our courts; our criminal justice system just lets them go. We literally risk our lives for others. I wonder if they'll ever understand? Every time a kid gets hurt, I relive my incident."

"Frank that's why we're writing this book. So they'll get a hint of what's going on."

Now we were both angry. "Frank, seven years for attempt murder? That should be a crime. Whoever made that decision should be prosecuted. They should go to prison. The damage they are doing to innocent people is incalculable. I had a case once when I was working detectives. It was a robbery kidnap case. I found the kidnapper and arrested him. What he had done was put a gun to the victim's head while she was sitting in her car. He shoved her aside to the passenger side. A second guy jumped in behind her. They drove her around and were hitting her in the head with a gun when she wasn't getting her jewelry off and handing it over fast enough. They let her out without killing her thank God. He was a hardcore gang member. Very hardcore. I got him the day after the robbery. The suspect had told me his aunt had given him the jewelry some years before. That statement indicated a consciousness of guilt. In my opinion, he should have at the least been charged with receiving stolen property. Did you know that even though he had the victim's jewelry, the district attorney wouldn't file charges against him? You know what the District Attorney told me?"

Frank had a look on his face like "try and surprise me."

"He said, 'Robert, it's the pea shooter principle.'"

"I asked the District Attorney, 'What's the pea shooter principle Al?'"

"You know a pea shooter only holds so many peas," he said. "A pea goes in another pea has to come out. Our prisons only hold so many peas. We can't put all of them in prison, they won't all fit."

I realized I had the same disgusted scowl on my face Frank had. He looked at me and said, "Lawyers… I went to court on the case. I didn't even testify. The guy pled out, thanks to the detectives' stellar investigation and the passengers' willingness to test-a-lie to save their own skin. The suspect's lawyer was the brother of a friend of mine. He wanted to say hello to me and introduce himself. Here he was willing to defend someone who had no problem killing complete strangers, and who tried to kill me. Then he had the gall to try to befriend the victim. Like it's nothing personal. Like it's no big deal. I wanted to tell him to get the hell away from me. Where is the conscience of people? Most lawyers have no conscience."

I completely understood it was an unspoken understanding between us. We had both lived it. "Do you still have the bullet in your arm?"

"No. It was bothering me, so they took it out several years later."

I didn't get much sleep for about week.

Chapter 3

The Mexican

Nadal St. and Whites Canyon Road, Santa Clarita, CA

She's not Mexican, but she might as well be. You will read how tough Mexicans can be in chapter five when they outrun Allan. Well Stacy is tougher than any Mexican I've ever met… EVAH!!

I did not know Stacy. How unfortunate for me. A friend of mine told me about her. When I met her I realized I'd missed something in my life. A genuinely good person. Honest, sincere, tough, unstoppable, and respectable are words that understate her. I want to call her the fudge lady because she will not cuss. As she tells her story it's, "Oh fudge I was in trouble," or "Oh Fudge he had a gun," or, "FUDGE IT HURT!" or just **"FUDGE!"** She does not drink. Imagine that, a gunfighter who died three times who does not drink or cuss.

I would say when she orders at a bar, she yells, **"Bartender! A glass of milk, and put a hair in it!"** but I don't think she goes to bars, unless there is someone in there shooting up the place. If that were the case, I have pity on the poor shooter.

When I first spoke to Stacy on the phone, I told her she would be my flower in the midst of all these stories by men. She laughed and asked me if it was because she was a woman? She then said, "I can be the flower in the midst of all the dandelions." So like her to take a weed and put a flower on it to make us ruffians just a little more palatable.

So why Mexican? She has the heart of a Mexican for one. For another a Mexican raised her. Nena was her neighbor who was every bit her second mom. She speaks of the love she shares with Mexican's love of tortillas. Of the sound of the masa slapping in Nena's hand as she made them in the morning as she was waking up. Of the smell of them while in bed, knowing soon she would be eating a fresh, warm, homemade tortilla with butter rolled up inside. The comfort and security in that simple event is evident in her smile as she talks about it. She talks of going to church with Nena every Sunday. She speaks of the deep love of family the Mexicans have, just like the Chinese.

Stacy is half Chinese, half Caucasian, but she might as well be Mexican. Like the guy who killed her three times.

*****

"Robert, a lot of people say, 'Woe is me.' Look, my parents divorced when I was five. I was raised by a single mom in the poor lower housing area in Tucson. I was split from my brothers and sisters growing up. Two of us went to live with my dad, and two of us with my mom. I was raised by a little Hispanic lady in my neighborhood while my mom worked in the copper mines of Tucson. My mom was a laborer digging up stuff in the mines. I was brought up to be self-sufficient from a young age. My mom would work different shifts. Often, we had to make our own dinner because mom was working until midnight or all-night long. But Nena was always that little old lady who lived downstairs, something stable in my life. Of course she was Spanish. People who are Spanish don't like to be called Mexican. I was taught that when I was really little. Nena used to say, I am Spanish, my husband is Mexican."

We both laughed. "She would make us tortillas. Anyone who is in bed and smells tortillas being made in the morning understands; it's awesome. On the way to school, you grab a tortilla, put a little butter in it and walk off to school eating your tortilla. It was cool because we lived in a Hispanic culture, a Hispanic area. Sometimes there would be six families living in a single house. The Mexican culture is a lot like the Asian culture, you know, you take care of the older family members, you respect them. I was blessed I had a caring little lady downstairs. She raised me like one of her own. She had two little boys. Her husband, Frank, worked as a mechanic; he was a hardworking man. I was the daughter he never had. It was a totally loving family, and I was the same as their daughter.

"We were poor, but we didn't think about it. I grew up with the kids in the neighborhood, and we often played outside. We would find a stick, and a ball and that was baseball. We had no mitts. Sometimes catching the ball really hurt. We'd point out a tree, and that would be first base. A rock would be second base. It was lots of fun, and I was really good. I grew up and played college softball. I loved that because it was a sense of family also. We were close. When I became a Los Angeles Police Officer, I played on their softball team. It was really cool to compete against other police and sheriff's departments because I got to know so many different people.

"Robert, to be a good cop you have to have compassion. You can be a cop without compassion, and you can get away with it. But you will not be a good cop. It's corny to say you came on the job to help protect those who cannot protect themselves, but it's true. To some people it's what's really in their heart. And to others who don't understand that, or feel that way, it sounds corny."

We smiled at each other. She was right.

"Stacy, I get the sense you always look on the bright side of things."

"Yeah I do. Sometimes you have to look really hard to find it," she started laughing, "But it's there, and if you can't put a little sunshine into someone's life what good is living? I think we were put on this earth to make everyone's life a little bit better, a little bit happier. By doing that you'll enrich your own life. It's sad for some people because the people who don't help others don't get that. They miss the point of living. Drugs, alcohol, those are temporary fixes. They don't fix the heart, the real problem. When you are growing up, you don't remember the money you had. You might remember a toy, but you really remember the times with your family, like picnics, even if you didn't really do anything special.

"I knew I wanted to be a cop since I was twelve years old. I was raised in Tucson, Arizona watching Adam 12 and Dragnet. I would tell people, and I know it sounds stupid, but I would tell them, 'That's what I'm going to be when I grow up.' There was never a doubt in my mind that's what the Lord had planned for me."

"Why?"

"When I used to watch *Adam 12* or *Dragnet* they were always protecting people who could not protect themselves. I never thought about how much money I could make. I always wanted to do something I and others could be proud of. I knew there was a path the Lord wanted me to walk. I wanted to work outside. I wanted to do something interesting and that was different every day. I wanted to help people and make a difference."

She smiled, "I just described law enforcement."

Stacy had a big grin on her face. "Patrol was always for me. Unlike detectives where you are handling cases, on patrol when you handle a call you're done. Then you get to go on another call. So I looked around and asked myself, 'Who's the biggest?' California Highway Patrol was big, but I didn't want to go around writing tickets my whole life. With the Sheriffs you had to go to work the jail after you graduate from the academy. I didn't want to go babysit anyone. L.A.P.D. had the reputation of being the best, so I figured I could learn the most from them. I wanted to be a little fish in a big pond and try to be, or emulate the best and biggest fishes. It bothers me sometimes when I see people look at police work as a job. I look at it as a something much more than that. Every single call you go on, you should do the best you can because people will remember that forever."

*****

"On Friday, June 8, 1990, I had been playing softball with the L.A.P.D. softball team. I actually got shot on June 9."

"I remember the date. Do you know why?"

"No."

"Because it's almost one year to the day before I got shot. I got shot on June 6, 1991. When I recently heard the date, you got shot I thought, 'Oh that's cool.' Not cool that you got shot, but that it was almost a year to the day before I got shot. I don't mean to say it was cool that we both got shot."

Stacy and I were laughing. She understood. "Yeah Robert we have something in common. It's that cop sense of humor a lot of people would never get. Because when I read your story, I thought, Oh, it was a year after I got shot he got shot."

Again we laughed. Similar minds.

"So after the Friday softball game, I would go to Shakey's with my friend Danny with his wife and kid. We would then go to his house and just hang out. It was a fairly common Friday night thing after softball we would get together. I remember that Friday we were watching *Big* with Tom Hanks. Usually I would stay over and sleep if it was late. However, that night I had to go to the station to turn in my time for the days I worked. If I didn't stay over, I always called him when I arrived home. I would let the phone ring one time that way he knew I was okay. That night when I left I went to the station and all the guys I worked with were there. I started talking and joking around and before you know it, it was midnight, and I realized I hadn't called Danny. I called Danny and let the phone ring one time so he wouldn't worry. I stuck around the station for another hour and talked some more with the guys and left.

I lived in Santa Clarita, close to the southeast corner of Nadal Street and Whites Canyon Road. It was a good thirty miles to my house from the station. It was one in the morning, I was tired, I was on autopilot. I just wanted to get home. I got home around one forty-five in the morning and parked in front of my house. From the front door of my house you could see my Bronco parked on the street. It was the city of Santa Clarita, right next to Canyon Country High School, it was a quiet neighborhood. Not a lot goes on there. So I had a ritual like all us coppers do, we consciously think of how we're going to get our gun from the car to the house so no one sees it and freaks out. If I was driving, I always carried my gun under my right leg. I had the barrel under my leg facing my left leg. That way if I needed it I could grab it quickly with my right hand."

"Stacy I carry mine under my left leg with the barrel facing the door. The gun butt is between my legs. If I carried my gun like you I would be afraid to shoot off my package. I don't want to accidentally shoot my package. I still need it!"

Again we laughed.

"Yeah that makes sense," she said with a huge grin. "So if it's daytime I will put my gun in a bag and carry it in the house. If it's night and dark, I will just grab my gun and put it under my left armpit then walk in the house. So after I parked I grabbed my gun, which was under my right leg. As I got out of the car, I had my gun in my right hand and was moving to put it under my left armpit as I simultaneously turned toward the rear of my Bronco. When I turned there was a guy with a gun pointed at me. I had not put the gun under my armpit yet, and so when I saw him, instead of putting my gun under my armpit, I aimed it at him. I was thinking, 'Police. Drop the gun,' and that's when it happened. I saw the cylinder of the gun with the bullets inside slowly turn. We were so close our guns could have been touching."

Ladies and gentlemen when a cylinder of a revolver turns it means the person holding the gun is pulling the trigger and the bullet in the cylinder is lining up with the barrel to be shot.

"That's when time slowed down. I knew he was going to fire the gun. I no longer saw him. I only saw the gun. I was looking down the barrel and it was huge. (Stacy put her hands up and made a circle with both hands, forefinger to forefinger, and thumb to thumb indicating the size of the barrel). I saw the bullets inside the cylinder, I could see it was a blue steel revolver and I saw this huge barrel pointed at me. And the cylinder was turning. I just got the word out, 'Police,' and he fired. It sounded like a cannon going off. The muzzle flash slowly expanded. Simultaneously I saw the bullet come out of the barrel."

"What?!"

"It's just like I'm standing here talking to you. Fudge, I see the bullet leave the gun and fly at me. It was a copper jacketed round. I could see the copper tip of the bullet with the muzzle flash of the gun behind it, and it was spinning straight toward me. I already had my gun in two hands, and when the bullet came at me I canted sideways pulling my right shoulder back, and then I fired. His bullet went right below my left breast and came out of my back and lodged in the inside of the car door. It was a 357 round and put a hole in my back the size of a tennis ball. The bullet slammed me into the door. When it slammed me into the door, the force of the bullet threw me so hard I bounced back onto my feet. Had it not been for the door the bullet would have knocked me to the ground."

Stacy was talking so fast she was skipping over things that really showed her character.

"Stacy, did it hurt?"

"Yeah, but things were happening really fast."

"Well it hurt. How?"

"It was like if you took a javelin and heated it up to a thousand degrees and stuck it through me... no drilled it through me, through my chest. That's what it felt like. I remember thinking, 'Fudge this is hot!'"

She started her story again. I stopped her from going on.

"Wait, wait," I said, "When did you start feeling the pain?"

"Oh it was instantaneous."

"What were you thinking?"

"Robert, I kept thinking it was so hot it *must* be searing and cauterizing everything that was in the path of the bullet. It never stopped feeling like that. It never stopped hurting. I was waiting for the pain to stop. I had been trained if you got shot, you'd feel pain. Then the adrenaline would kick in, and you wouldn't feel the pain anymore. Then you could get the job done. I was waiting for the adrenaline to kick in to stop the pain. That never happened. Fudge it hurt so bad, it was so hot, so searingly hot and it never stopped. But I knew I had a job to do. It wasn't over yet. I thought, 'This kid's shooting at me. I've got to stop this guy or he's going to hurt somebody else.' I was angry. I was thinking, 'HOW DARE YOU SHOOT ME, I'M A POLICE OFFICER!' I was thinking I had identified myself as a police officer, you're supposed to respect my authority and not shoot me.

"After he and I shot, he turned and ran to the back of my Bronco. I thought, 'Oh no you don't, you son of a gun. You can't shoot me then run through my neighborhood and think you're going to get away.' I was thinking it hurts, but if the kid is going to shoot a police officer he'll shoot anyone and I'm not going to let that happen. I never had it in my head I was going to hunt him down and kill him. I was thinking I had to stop him from hurting anyone else. I was thinking I've got to protect the neighbors from this kid. He's going to kill someone. Your job doesn't stop when you go home. Your heart of being a police officer is the same.

"When he got to the rear of the Bronco he turned left behind it. I took a couple of steps to chase him and realized I couldn't see him. So, as I got to the rear of the Bronco, I stopped and started edging around the corner of the car to see if he was there. As I leaned right, he was kneeling on the ground waiting for me. We saw each other. He raised his gun and pointed it at me. Instantly I leaned just a little left and fired at the same time he fired. (Here Stacy told me of her conscious thought process of how she methodically and tactically shot to ensure placing rounds into the threat.) He fired five more shots at me. I could see each muzzle flash of his gun firing, but I never heard it. He emptied his gun. He missed all five shots. As he was firing, I shot three times. Here's the thing, although I couldn't hear his gunshots, I heard mine. He crumpled to the street. I could see he was out of the fight. I reached up to my chest and could feel I was wet. I looked at my hand and saw blood. I thought all the blood should be behind me because I had felt the bullet come out of my back, but it wasn't. I don't know why but I must have had it in my mind when your blood is outside of your body it should be cold. When I felt my chest, my blood was warm, and that's how I realized it was mine, and it was coming out warm. I went, 'FUDGE I'm bleeding. Dang it! That's my blood, I've got to get to the house to get some help.' I went to the front of my Bronco. When I got to the hood, I stopped. I pointed my gun to the passenger side of the car to make sure there wasn't a second suspect waiting. It was clear.

"I started walking up my driveway. I got three or four steps and realized, 'Oh oh…Fudge Stace, you're going to pass out.' I didn't want to fall on my face because I knew I would smash my face up. I was worried if I smashed up my face, then after the doctors finished fixing me up I would look really bad." She started giggling. "I didn't want to mess up my face, so before I passed out, I got on my knees and rolled onto my back and passed out from there."

"You'd been shot, you shot him. Then you rounded your Bronco, he fired at you five more times. You fired three times. You had a thousand-degree javelin through your chest. You had warm blood pumping out of your chest. You had a tennis-ball-sized hole in your back…and you were worried about your face?"

"Yeah, it's weird the things that go through your mind. Hee-hee."

*****

"The Lord took care of me. The reason I say this is because he took the memories away of what they did to save me."

*****

"A week later I woke up in the hospital. The Dodger game was on. Danny was there. I looked at him, 'What happened?'"

"'You did great kid. You did great. Get some rest.' I was out again."

"Stacy, were you ever scared or think you were going to die?"

"No, I believe the Lord in some way let me know I was going to come back. I knew I was going to be sore, but I knew I wasn't going to die. The hardest part of this whole thing was seeing the faces of those I loved after I came back. I could see they had believed I was going to die, and they had gone through terrible pain. That hurt me more than anything else.

"I lost a week of my life. I have no recollection of that time. But subconsciously I was communicating with people. A week before I got shot I took a class in sign language. So when I was unconscious that week, I was signing names with my hand of the people I wanted to see.

I wanted to know what happened but no one would tell me because I hadn't spoken to the shooting team yet. I told Danny, 'Send them in, I want to know what happened.' I thought I had initially fired twice, but the shell casings showed I fired once, then three more times. The department said I was out of policy by carrying my gun in my car unholstered. Robert, if that had happened, I never would have been able to shoot the suspect. It takes two hands to unholster your gun if you are not wearing it." She laughed, "Imagine getting the Medal of Valor, and then getting disciplined for having your gun unholstered?"

I think Stacy was kidding, but I wasn't sure. She was grinning as she said this.

"Robert, this is where the story starts. One of my roommates was a dispatcher for the L.A.P.D. She heard the shots but thought someone in the neighborhood was shooting off fireworks. So she came outside to yell out, 'Hey knock it off it's one forty-five in the morning,' and she sees my car parked in the street. She can see the driver's door open with the dome light on. She's looking around for me and wondering where I am. So she starts down the walkway, and she sees me laying in the driveway. She runs back in the house and calls 911. She said all the right things and gets help on the way. There was an L.A.P.D. officer named Steve who lived right up the street. She called him and told him I'd been shot and he needed to come over right away. Steve came over in his pajamas and slippers with his gun and badge. Steve drove up, and as he turned the corner, he saw the kid I shot in the street at the back of the Bronco. He stopped in the middle of the street and checked him. He was dead. He then ran over to me and took my gun, which had fallen out of my hand. He realized it was evidence, but also realized the paramedics would be working on me and he wanted the gun out of the way. My gun had stovepiped. (This is where a bullet casing does not fully eject from the pistol after the bullet is fired. The casing is stuck at the slide and stops the next bullet from feeding into the barrel. Basically the gun is jammed and inoperable. This usually happens when the shooter does not have a firm grip on the gun as they shoot, known as limp-wristing.) I think it was because I was losing all that blood and I had a weak grip on the gun when I fired my last shot. I never knew my gun had stovepiped.

"A Los Angeles County Sheriff's Deputy (this area is patrolled by the Los Angeles County Sheriff's Department), was right down the hill and was there really quick. The Los Angeles County Fire Department Station was right down the hill, and the paramedics were there quickly also. They put a mast suit around my legs, which inflates and creates pressure. They wanted to move blood to my chest to get my organs filled with blood. While they were working on me, I lost my pulse. My heart had stopped working. They defibrillated me several times and got my pulse back. They rushed me to the hospital. There was a new shift of doctors coming on duty. I basically had two sets of surgeons working on me. One of the doctors, Doctor Macabee, was a Vietnam vet doctor who had a lot of experience with gunshot victims. When they went in, they found the bullet had fragmented and nicked my diaphragm and shattered my spleen. It went through my liver, stomach, large and small intestine; it put a hole in the base of my heart, and it cracked the rib as it went out of my back. It missed my lung, and it missed my kidney. Fortunately, the doctors went in and just sewed everything up. Except for my spleen; they had to take it out. They called in a heart specialist, and Macabee put his finger in the hole in my heart until the specialist could get there to sew it up. I was on about 75 percent life support in the Intensive Care Unit.

"While in the Intensive Care Unit, my heart stopped again. They had to defibrillate me again and bring me back. I was going through too much blood. The L.A.P.D. Metro Unit was collecting blood from the Red Cross and taking it to Los Angeles County Medical Center. They then transported it by helicopter to my hospital. They didn't know why I was losing so much blood and decided they had to go back in and open me up again to find where I was bleeding. This was about an hour after my first surgery, while I was still in recovery. Doctor Macabee came to me and told me they had to open me up again, but since I had just come out of surgery and was still in recovery, they couldn't give me any anesthesia. They couldn't put me under. He asked me to squeeze his fingers if I understood. I did.

"I don't remember any of this.

"By this time, they had gotten a hold of Danny whose phone I had called earlier and let ring one time to let him know I was home and okay. When he got the call, he learned I had been shot and had not made it home. When they wheeled me into the second surgery, he was already at the hospital. He later told me, 'Stacy, when they wheeled you into surgery, you were dead. I've seen a lot of dead bodies, and you were dead. There was no way you were coming out a second time.'

"When they took me into surgery the second time my heart went into full arrest. I was opened up when this happened. Doctor Macabee reached his hand into my chest and manually massaged my heart. He did this for the next forty-five minutes. Doctor Macabee has since told me I was dead. He knew he could not save me. My heart had completely stopped working. The only reason he continued with the heart massage, is he wanted my parents to be able to get to the hospital with me still alive. After forty-five minutes he stopped, and then my heart started. He told me no way was that possible, I was dead. He wholeheartedly believes the Lord made it happen. He said he is not a religious man, but that made him believe in divine intervention.

"They found an artery had been nicked and was still bleeding. They sewed it up then sewed me up. I was now on 100 percent life support. My family was now at the hospital. L.A.P.D. had flown my mom up from Arizona, then after landing at Burbank Airport, they flew her in a helicopter to me. The doctors told them I was on 100 percent life support, and the machines were keeping me alive. They said at best I only had several hours to live. They all got together and prayed, 'Lord, if you want her, take her, if not, bring her back.'

"I later heard my family was in my room. My mom was yelling at me telling me she didn't raise a quitter. My family was telling me if I understood them to move my finger or toe. And I would respond to them. This was about an hour into my second recovery. They told the doctor I was responding. He said he would go into the room, but wanted them to know when the body shuts down, it is normal for the toes and fingers to twitch. He had no hope I would survive. But, when he went to my room, he saw I was responding to him also. He told my family, 'She's fighting back.' My dad had been picked up by some officers and driven to the hospital. He was a mess, I was his baby daughter. My sister and my brother were there and they were all telling me to fight. But I don't remember any of it.

"All the brass from the department came to see me. I was the first female officer shot in the history of the department, and it looked like I was going to be the first to be killed.

"I had officers assigned to guard me. I had killed a gang member. They were concerned a fellow gang member might try to kill me. In addition to this, the gang member that shot me happened to be a gang member in the area where I worked. They thought it was possibly a hit against me because I was an officer in the area. It turned out this wasn't the case. The news put out the shooting happened in front of my house and they gave the location. So now everyone there had to be moved out in case a fellow gang member wanted to kill my family members or friends I lived with."

Just for the record, Stacy nor any of her roommates still live at the location.

*****

"Chief Gates came to the hospital and brought me a case of Pepsi. That was cool. He knew that's what I drank. He told me when I got well I could work anywhere I wanted. I had my choice.

"I told him, 'I want to work Southeast morning watch, (eleven p.m. to seven a.m.).'"

I started laughing. Folks, if you don't know Los Angeles, the Los Angeles Police Southeast Division is one of the busiest stations in the city. I know, I worked in the county area that borders this division. There were six murders my first week on patrol. "Why? Stacy, why?" I asked her.

She started laughing with me. "Gates looked at me," she now was whispering and leaning into me like a little conspiracy; she was imitating her conversation with Chief Gates, 'Stacy you can go…anywhere,' she leaned in closer to me imitating him again, her eyebrows lower and her voice got even lower… 'anywhere.'

"I told him, 'Chief I know, but I joined to be a police officer. If I can't work Southeast and become the best, I can't prove to you I am the best.' He said, 'Okay, just let me know when you are ready.'

"Fifteen days after being admitted to the hospital, I went home. I was under house arrest. Doctor's orders. I stayed with my dad. He was worried I would not obey the doctor. My dad called Chief Gates on his personal cell phone, 'I'm worried Stacy will leave the house.'

"The Chief asked if he could assign an officer to stay with me. My dad requested Danny. So, Danny became my babysitter. A Southeast morning-watch, hard-charging cop now had to babysit me. I would basically ring a bell and order room service. Sandwiches, multiple cans of Pepsi on ice, whatever my heart desired. Danny kept doing the maid service thing all the while telling me there would be payback.

"Eight months later I was partnered up with Danny at Southeast Division. He said it was now time for payback. He said he wanted a cup of coffee, hot and black waiting for him every night when he arrived at briefing. Fudge, I had to get him coffee every day before shift and put it on the table in front of where he sat. We ended up being partners for five years. And he was a training officer. He should have been partnered with a probationer, but no one was going to tell Chief Gates we couldn't be partners.

"I refused to let a fifteen-year-old gangbanger determine my career. This was my passion. I never went through the psychological things like what's it like to kill someone. I actually had worse injuries than he did. But I survived. He didn't. I had the will to survive. He didn't. He called the shots, not me. I reacted to the set of circumstances he set up, and I won. You do what you have to do to protect your life or someone else's life. He made the call. I didn't. I feel bad for the mom, she no longer has her son, but I didn't make that decision, he did."

*****

"Five people were looking to steal a car that night. Five Mexican gang members. Prior to following me on the freeway, they had been following two other cars. The first car they followed got pulled over by the California Highway Patrol. Obviously, they stopped following them.

They lost the second car in a neighborhood. I was the third car. I never saw them following me. They said they followed me for about thirty miles. When I parked in front of my house on Nadal, they were northbound on Whites Canyon Road behind me. They stopped and let the fifteen-year-old gang member out of the car along with his fourteen-year-old girlfriend. The twenty-year-old gang member who was the driver, pulled a U-turn and parked facing south on Whites Canyon Road just south of Nadal. In the car was the fourteen-year-old girlfriend of the other girl. She was babysitting her eleven-year-old brother who wanted to be a gang member. Five people total. The oldest was twenty. The youngest eleven.

"The reason they were going to steal a car? It was because the fourteen-year-old girlfriend told her fifteen-year-old boyfriend if he loved her, he would steal a car for her. So, he stole his mother's 357 revolver, and all five-people got into a car to steal another.

"When the fifteen-year-old got out, he immediately went to the driver's side of my car. His girlfriend went to the passenger side. When I got out, there he was pointing his gun at me. After the shooting, the girl jumped into some neighbor's bushes. That's why I never saw her after shooting her boyfriend. Right after the shooting the twenty-year-old, seeing what had happened, drove off with the fourteen-year-old girl and her eleven-year-old brother.

"After the Los Angeles County Sheriff's Deputies had locked down the neighborhood, the girl in the bushes came out and went and sat on the curb. While they were checking with neighbors for any possible witnesses, one of them pointed out the girl sitting on the curb. The neighbor had seen her come out of the bushes.

"She gave up all the information. When the deputies detained her she said, referring to the dead fifteen-year-old, 'That's my boyfriend who the officer shot.'

"They asked her how she knew I was an officer. She said she heard me say 'police' before the shooting started.

"She told them the reason she went with the fifteen-year-old was she knew how to drive a stick shift. My Bronco was a stick shift, and the plan was she was going to drive it away after stealing it.

"It was later determined the mother of the fifteen-year-old had been having trouble with her son for five years. Since he'd been about ten. She could not control him. He already had numerous detentions (juveniles do not get arrested in California, they get detained). He had a record. The fourteen-year-old girlfriend had a record. The twenty-year-old had a record. Everyone blamed the crime on the fifteen-year-old. Of course, when you're dead you can't deny anything.

"Everyone was in custody within three hours.

"The fifteen-year-old was dead. The twenty-year-old got ten years for assault with a deadly weapon on a police officer, attempted robbery and grand theft auto. Both fourteen-year-old girls got probation and the eleven-year-old got nothing."

*****

Ladies and gentlemen, people always think if a police officer identifies him or herself, then the problem is over; who would dare shoot a police officer? This story so plainly illustrates this is not the case. People need to understand sometimes it is a war and it is them or us. We shoot out of necessity and out of reverence for life. Oftentimes the news portrays these people shot by the police as innocents. Or us as bloodthirsty thugs. Nothing is further from the truth. They leave out or fail to get the real story or the true lifestyle of the person shot. It's all meant to sensationalize these events to sell more news time. By the news failing to get the "full story" or by only interviewing family members, who never tell about their poor son's drug use or gang affiliations, they do you and I a severe disservice. This turns us who try to genuinely help, and you who want to believe in us, against each other. It should not be that way.

*****

In 1991, Stacy was inducted into the American Police Officer Hall of Fame as the officer of the year. "That was pretty cool. But what was really cool was they gave me a five-day working cruise. I had to agree to attend some classes.

"I said, 'Let me get this straight. I get to go on a cruise, all expenses paid, and the only thing I have to do is attend a few classes?'

"They said 'right.'

"I said, 'I'm there!' And they let me bring someone. When Southeast Division heard about it, I had all these guys lined up wanting to go with me. I told them, 'If you get your wife to tell me personally it is okay I'll take you.' No takers, not one of them did it!" She and I were laughing. "I took Nena. She had never been on a cruise before. Never really been anywhere, not even out of Tucson."

*****

From the time the suspect pointed the gun at Stacy till the time she passed out was about five seconds.

*****

Stacy now teaches tactics for the Los Angeles Police Department.

Stacy Lim was awarded the Purple Heart after the Los Angeles Police Department instituted it for officers injured in the line of duty.

Stacy Lim also received the Medal of Valor for her actions on the night of June 9, 1990. It is the highest award the Los Angeles Police Department can bestow upon its officers.

Chapter 4

South Ontario

Sultana Ave. and Park St., Ontario, CA

Mike told me he had felt wetness right above his belly button. Terrified to look at his stomach, he touched it instead. When he pulled his hand away, he looked at his fingers. What he saw horrified him. He couldn't understand. It was supposed to be blood.

His next words sickened and chilled me.

*****

Mike grew up in Oxnard, California. His father was a World War II and Korean War veteran.

He grew up in a white area. Just like me. In fact, he was like me in so many ways. Mexican like me, but whiter. He learned Spanish in school, he grew up in a middle-class home, he married at nineteen-years-old, he had a son, he divorced his wife seven years later, he remarried, and they were white women. All eerily like me.

We connected instantly. Mike has the same sarcastic, quick sense of humor I do. If you ever got a hold of Mike's home phone number and had to leave a message, you would hear one of his grandchildren answering and apologizing for the family not being available. Mike loves his family and his grandchildren.

He is just a great, fun loving guy.

*****

"Robert, I started working as a dishwasher. When I got married, I was working as a cook actually making dinners at a restaurant. But I had a wife and a son on the way, and I needed more money. I got a job in a meat packing company warehouse from 1974 to 1977. The problem was from November to February of those years, things would slow down and I would be laid off. For the first three years of my son's life, we had to go to my parent's home so we could have Christmas presents. My little family was on Medi-Cal, I was on unemployment. The meat packing job was a union job, and sometimes during the time I was laid off, I would get called back into work. I would work for a week, then get laid off again. I would have to re-apply for unemployment and wait for it to get approved. A month would go by with very little money. It was very stressful and scary. I realized I needed something more stable.

"In January 1977, I was attending Long Beach State University trying to finish my Administration of Justice bachelor's degree. I already had my Associates of Science degree from Ventura Community College. I was working graveyards at the meat packing plant, and it just wasn't working. My grades were in the tank. When I got laid off in 1977, I decided I needed a real job.

"The funny thing is everything I learned in college had nothing to do with real life police work. If I had operated the way the college taught me to operate, I would have been killed a hundred times over. Everything I learned about being a cop I learned in the academy and from my training officers. The courses in college were all about how law enforcement was failing. They had these great theories on how to rehabilitate people. They taught that this plan or that plan needed to be implemented and these plans would cut down crime. The truth is when we go out there, we are hands-on with violent criminals. Sometimes we kill people, and sometimes we get hurt. That is the reality. There is no theory when you are facing a gun. The teachers were all about getting a job with the federal government as an agent. They would tell us, 'You don't want to spend your degree being a street cop. You want to spend your degree making the real money, with the Feds, (Federal Government).'

My older brother was an A.B.C. agent (State of California Alcohol Beverage and Control), and he was having a lot of fun. I have relatives with the United States Marshals Department and with the Department of Labor." Mike laughed, "No money. They don't make the good money."

*****

"I got hired by the Ontario Police Department and went through the San Bernardino County Sheriff's Training Academy in 1977. After I was hired, the patrol captain pulled me into his office and welcomed me. He told me straight out, 'We hired you because you are a Mexican who speaks English well and can write well. We need you because the Mexicans in the south end are killing everybody. We need you to go down there and help us figure it out.'

"You know Robert, today a lot of people would be upset with that introduction, but hell, I was happy to have a job, and I appreciated his honesty and candor. And as the years went on, I would have followed this captain into hell to do battle.

"Robert, in the late seventies the Inland Empire was still like the Wild West. The wave of professionalism in law enforcement had just started moving from Los Angeles, east toward us, but it was still developing. In 1977, the whole west end of the Inland Empire was involved in a massive gang war. The street gangs were trying to establish their connections with the Mexican Mafia out of Chino's men's prison. If they could ally themselves with the Mexican Mafia, it would give them a chunk of the money stemming from illegal activity. So, the Mexican Mafia was allowing the street gangs to kill each other. They wanted the strongest, and that's who they were going to use as their street gang presence. And the gangs were killing each other. They were all Mexican street gangs. It was the Ontario Black Angels versus the Cucamonga Kings versus the Chino Sinners. They battled it out for supremacy. Talk about brutal, they would hang a body on a barbed wire fence then shoot it up. A farmer would find it hanging on his fence the next day. Our police administration didn't understand what was going on in South Ontario. I know it sounds weird in today's time and age, but all the civilians were intimidated by these gangs. We would have witnesses to shootings who were standing eight or ten feet away from each other who never saw anything. The people in South Ontario were scared.

"Just to let you know the intensity of the crime, within 18 months three of us were shot. And they were luring us in. Ambushing us. In retaliation for my shooting, some gang members set a lumberyard on fire. When our officer responded, he started directing traffic in the street. A gang member hiding in the smoke shot him in both legs from across the street. The gang had set the lumberyard on fire to get an officer in the middle of the street so they could shoot and kill him. The last shooting was when a gang member lured an officer into a foot pursuit. When the officer ran through a park chasing the suspect, his fellow gang members started sniping at him with a .22 caliber rifle. A bullet fragmented on the park's chain-link fence, and he was shot in the head. Luckily it was a fragment, the round did not penetrate his skull.

"The south of Ontario was a very condensed population of low-income Mexican families, some good… some not so good.

"On August 25, 1979, I had just started my shift. I was working a one-man unit, and my shift was from 11:00 p.m. to 7:00 a.m. After briefing, I was getting my radio car ready and noticed my driver's spotlight wasn't working. So, I was in the mechanic bay looking for tools so I could change out my light. Right then the station got a call of a man who had just been shot. My sergeant yelled out, 'Let's go!' I jumped in my radio car and drove off into the Wild West. What had happened was two male Mexicans went in the back door of the Mac's Merri-Den Bar. They were both armed. One was armed with a sawed-off shotgun. The other had a handgun. While the one with the shotgun waited by the back door and covered the bar, the other was busy robbing all the drunken patrons. It just so happened the backdoor was next to the men's bathroom. The bathroom had two side-by-side swinging saloon doors you see in the western movies. A fat, drunk patron, unaware of what was going on, pushed the swinging door and hit the Mexican gunman. The Mexican panicked and swung his shotgun around, pointing it at the fat drunk and fired. Thank God the shotgun only had birdshot (this is a shotgun load used to hunt birds, and is not as powerful as Buckshot or .00, double-aught shot). The blast hit the patron and blew him back into the toilet. Thank God again the drunk was so fat, because the shotgun pellets only penetrated the poor drunk's fat. No vital organs were hit, and he survived. Guess what the description of the robbers was?"

"Oh, I don't know Mike. Let me guess… Ahhh, two male Mexicans?"

"Geez, Robert you are so smart!!! Two male Mexicans wearing bandanas. I knew everyone was going to the bar, so I went hunting in the street. I was a hot dog officer with mustard and ketchup (a hot dog is someone always in the action). I knew the action there was over, and I'd probably end up on traffic control. That's not me, I hated traffic control. There were bad guys to catch. I was looking for the robbery suspects and driving around the south end of Ontario.

"At 11:26 p.m. I was driving west on Park Street, I was east of Sultana Ave. This was about 11 blocks away from the shooting. A two-door 1963 Chevrolet Impala was driving east on Park Street approaching me, they were west of Sultana Ave. The intersection of Park and Sultana has a four-way stop sign. The Chevy got to Sultana Ave. and the driver must have seen me approaching west on Park out of the dark because he abruptly stopped after a quarter of his car passed the stop sign limit line. Too late for him, I had a traffic violation. As we crossed the intersection passing each other, I could see the right rear passenger. I knew him as an Ontario Black Angel gang member. The word on the street was he had committed numerous assaults with deadly weapons and he had killed a few people. I made a U-turn and pulled in quickly behind them. We were now going east on Park Street just east of Sultana Ave. There were six people in the car, the driver, a woman who was in the front passenger seat with a baby on her lap, a guy behind the driver, a rear passenger in the middle, and the right rear passenger, the gang member I knew.

"The Chevy was driving very slowly. I could tell they were trying to do everything right to not violate any vehicle laws, so I would not stop them. I lit them up (turned on the overhead red lights to pull them over). We had just passed the first house when I lit them up. Instead of pulling over to the right, the driver made a left turn into a driveway that had a closed chain-link gate. The gate bordered the sidewalk. The gate blocked the Chevy from going up the driveway into the house's front yard. I parked my unit at a slight angle to the driver's left rear bumper and hit the high beams. My unit was sticking out into Park Ave. and blocking the north part of the street. Their car was blocked between the closed gate and the front of my radio unit. The Chevy's doors were right over the sidewalk. I opened my driver's door, and while keeping an eye on them, I let dispatch know where I was. I asked for a backup unit and asked dispatch to run the plate."

Mike then repeated the plate to me, just as if he was running the plate at the time this occurred. I looked at Mike incredulously, "Mike this was over thirty years ago. How in the world do you still remember the plate?"

Mike smiled at me, "Robert, I used to lecture on my shooting for years at the academy. I've heard the tape a million times. I know the plate by heart.

"As soon as I finished putting out I wanted backup, the middle rear passenger, who I did not recognize, climbed over the Ontario Black Angel who I did know, and got out of the right passenger door. He started walking east on the north side of Park Street, away from the car. Even though it was a very hot August night, he was wearing a black trench coat. I quickly walked in between the front of my radio car and the rear of the Chevy. As he continued walking into the darkness, I yelled, 'Hey hold it right there! Stop.' I could see everyone in the car bobbing around, looking at him, looking at me, and looking around. I thought to myself, 'Oh, Goddammit!' I knew I was in a bad position. The suspect was about eight feet away from the car when I got to him. My back was now to the Chevy. I told you I was a hot dog. Maybe too much so. I had these people behind me now, one of which I believed was a killer. But my impulse was to get the guy, the suspect, who was walking away. He was guilty of something. The suspect and I were now on the sidewalk, and he was standing with his back to me facing east. Behind me was all lit up with my headlights, but the suspect and I were in the darkness. He was looking down the street into the dark, then he looked back at me, then into the dark again. I felt he wanted to run, but I don't know why he didn't. I looked at him, and then I looked at the car. When I got to him, I was no longer looking at him but was looking at the car. I knew the right rear passenger was a gang member who had probably committed some murders. I reached out and put my right hand on the back of his right elbow. I started turning him so he would be completely facing away from me. I moved his arm about six inches. I was just reaching around with my left arm to start patting him down when he suddenly spun to his right. As he spun, he jerked his right elbow backward, breaking the contact I had on him. Feeling his resistance, I started turning my gaze from the Chevy back to him. He was now sideways, at a right angle to me.

"Robert, understand all this happened in less than a second. He then yelled, **'THAT'S IT FUCKER!'** Mind-numbing panic hit me like a ton of bricks, **'OH SHIT I CAN'T SEE HIS HANDS!!!'** I grabbed my gun. In his left hand at waist level, he was holding a gun. How do I know this, even though I didn't see it? I know because three things happened simultaneously. I heard a cannon-like sound, **'BOOOM!!!'** lightning blew up in my face, and a huge sledgehammer hit my stomach. I was hit one inch above my belly button. I didn't know it at the time, but I had been shot with a .41 magnum handgun. When these three things happened, reality immediately went into slow motion. It was like a picture frame sequence. Everything was like a slow-motion movie, with frames of what was happening passing in front of me. There was no fluid movement of life. It was all clicks of a picture roll. I realized I couldn't see his hands, and when he shot me, it knocked me back half a step. When I got knocked back, it jerked my hand, which was pulling my gun out of the holster. I fired. I saw a silhouette in front of me but off to the side, floating down. The sound his gun made when fired was *'BOOOOOM!!!'* and mine was 'pop?' I was looking at the car because I worried about the gang member in the rear seat. So, I was firing while looking at the car, trying desperately to move my head to face the suspect. Things had slowed down so much it seemed like an eternity. Out of the corner of my eye, I could see the suspect disappearing and falling, floating downward as a shadow, a silhouette."

"Mike, your threat was in front of you… **shooting you!**"

"Robert, I know. We were firing at each other from eighteen inches away, but from the beginning, I had it in my mind the guy behind me was the threat. I was really worried about him. I was in a shitty position. I had bad guys in front of me and behind me."

Mike hadn't read my story, "Mike I understand."

Mike started laughing, "I was the meat to that sandwich!"

I started laughing too, having been there.

"When I fired my second shot, 'pop?' I was feeling pain in my stomach. I was still looking at the car now but turning my head, and all I could see was a blur of motion as the passengers in the car were ducking below the windows. I fired again, 'pop?' The three rounds I fired were almost like one shot, but as you can see a lot was going on between each shot. Pop pop pop. And although they were like one shot, in my mind each shot was taking about a minute to complete. I know it doesn't make sense, and it is impossible for someone to understand unless you have experienced it. Things were happening very fast and very slow, all at the same time. The best way to describe it is my arm was fast, but my mind was slowing everything down."

I understood.

"Mike, could you hear your shots?"

Mike looked at me as if suddenly realizing something very profound, "Nope. I had no idea I fired my gun…no idea I fired my gun. I know it sounds like a contradiction because I just said I heard my gun go pop three times very quickly, but then seemed like each shot took a minute. I guess at the time it happened I didn't hear it. But thinking back on it I did. It's the fog of war. Soldiers try to explain it all the time. When lawyers hear this stuff, they say the officer is untruthful because his statements are contradictory. However, it's not that the officer is being untruthful. It's how it happened as he remembered it. All I can say is at the time it happened I didn't hear my gun, but later I knew the rounds sounded like they were fired like one shot. But as I was shooting, it seemed like each shot took a minute. Time and my hearing were distorted at different levels all at the same time. I didn't know I shot my gun until milliseconds later."

"Then how did you figure out you fired?"

"After my third round goes off, he was gone in the darkness. I couldn't see him. And try as I might I couldn't find him. It was like I was in a dark room. And I couldn't see him. It was confusing. A millisecond before he was there. I turned back from the car, and now he was gone. Like he vanished into thin air. How did that happen?

"I looked down, and I could see my gun. It was hot. How did that happen? I could feel the heat from my gun in my hand. I said to myself, 'I gotta get out of here.' Then I realized, 'I've been shot, **'FUCK I'VE BEEN SHOT!'** I hadn't realized I'd been shot.

"I started running back to my radio car. When I was about ten feet from the unit's passenger side, I heard, *'BOOOM!'* behind me. **'MOTHER-FUCKER HE'S STILL SHOOTING AT ME!!!'** my head screamed at me. I kept running. When I got to the rear of the radio car I hear again, **'BOOOM!!!'** He missed me both times. When he fired his third shot, I could see the muzzle flash of his gun. The muzzle flash illuminated him for an instant, and I could see he was lying on the ground and firing at me sideways. He was firing from the same location where I had grabbed him, from where he first fired. I was trying to pull my radio out of my belt to put out a call for help, but I still had my flashlight in my hand, and I couldn't do both. I dropped my flashlight and put out, 'I've been shot, I've been shot. Paul-4 (Paul-4 was the unit identifier he was assigned that night), I've been shot.' At this point, eleven seconds had gone by since the time I put out a call for backup.

"Now I'm pissed. I want to kill him. To say that is really an understatement. I had decided one of us was going to die. I was thinking, 'I'm hurt, you're hurt. Otherwise, you would be running.' But he was lying on the sidewalk shooting at me.

"I walked away from my radio car into the middle of the street, and I start shooting at him. My fourth round hit the rear of their car. The fifth round went through his trench coat and into the ground. My sixth round went somewhere off into space, never to be seen again. And then I'm empty. I'm out of bullets. I'm standing there in the open, silhouetted behind by lights from a bakery across the street, pulling my trigger and clicking an empty gun. I couldn't believe it. I stood there in the street and looked at my gun cursing it. **BOOOM!!!'** He shot at me for the fourth time.

"I was looking at my gun and thought, 'I need to reload.' Then I realized I had not practiced reloading since the academy. I had no faith in my ability to do this. I had drop pouches, which contained bullets. The tops of them had become warped. I knew they wouldn't work correctly. I knew I was going to have to pull each bullet out one at a time and feed it into the gun and do it under fire, after being shot, with adrenaline surging through my body, making my hands shake. It was going to take too much time. Time I didn't have. I had a backup gun, but I had trained myself to believe my backup was to shoot someone if they grabbed my primary weapon. During this whole incident, I never even considered using my backup. I thought…'Get the shotgun.'

"As I ran to the driver's door to get the shotgun, **'BOOOM!!!'** He fired a fifth shot. As I'm running, I'm trying to get my gun back into my holster, and I couldn't get it in. Too much adrenaline. I dropped the gun at the left rear tire of my car, and it kicked off my foot, landing under my radio car. So now, I have eighteen live bullets on my belt, and I have no gun. I got the shotgun, and racked a live round into the chamber (racking a round in the shotgun means you have worked the slide on the shotgun and mechanically fed a shotgun shell from the holding chamber to the firing chamber. In effect, you have placed a live load containing pellets into the firing chamber).

"Robert, racking that shotgun was the sweetest sound in the world. I knew he had a big gun by the sound it was making. But now I had **'THE BIG FUCKING GUN!'** I ran right around the back of the car, right into the open. Right in the middle of the street. I wanted to have a clear, unobstructed shot at him. **'You want to fight motherfucker? One of us is going to die!'** I was so pissed it was unbelievable. I got down on one knee, I put the bead of the shotgun on him, on the black fucking silhouette on the ground. Up came his hand with the gun. I had him, and I couldn't miss. The trigger clicked. I had pulled it… click. Nothing. Nothing happened. It didn't fire. The round was a dud. **FUUUUCK!** Frustrated beyond frustrated I was grinding my teeth in exasperation. I racked another round in the shotgun, I made sure the safety was off, I got on target again…and then it happened. The suspect threw his gun. He waved his hand at me like, 'I give up, I give up.' My finger was tense on the trigger; I was going to fire, but then the cop in me kicked in. I couldn't do it. I couldn't kill him. I wanted to so badly, but I couldn't.

"The pain in my stomach then hit me hard! OH MY GOD! I'd never felt such pain in my life. Time immediately went back to normal. I duck-walked back to my radio car and put the safety on the shotgun. I leaned it against the unit. I sat on the ground leaning up against the right rear tire of my unit. I felt wetness on my stomach. I put my hand there and pulled it away looking at my fingers. I was horrified. It should have been blood. When you get shot, you're supposed to bleed. I wasn't bleeding. It was a clear gooey fluid with flecks of red in it. 'Oh my God what is that?' I was terrified. I took a handkerchief from my front pocket and had placed it over my stomach. I was afraid to look.

"Robert, did you see the movie *The New Centurions?*"

"Yes Mike, I did." And then in unison we both said, "Stacey Keach."

Folks if you have never seen *The New Centurions* it is a movie taken from the book written by Joseph Wambaugh from the same title. In the movie, the actor Stacy Keach who plays a cop gets shot in the stomach with a shotgun. After being shot he rolls over and you could see his intestines coming out of his stomach.

"Robert, that's why I put the hanky over my stomach. I didn't want my guts spilling out into the street.

"While I sat there two of my partners had been rolling to my initial call for backup. One of the officers had seen me running around shooting but couldn't see the suspect. He didn't know where the suspect was. The officer was on foot, stealthily approaching the car westbound from the sidewalk. The other officer got to me where I sat.

"Mikey, are you okay, are you okay?"

"I'm shot."

"Can you walk?"

"I don't know?"

"Okay, stay with me."

"He hooked both of his arms under my armpits and dragged me to the opposite side of the car where I had cover.

"I yelled out to the other officer, 'It's the motherfucker in the trench coat!' As this officer was approaching and concentrating on the car, he almost tripped on something on the ground. It was the suspect. It was so dark he never saw him. The suspect was on the ground gurgling in his own blood.

"The fire department was very close. The paramedics got there. It was Ed. This paramedic was known by all the cops for saving people. I was so glad to see him.

"When Ed got to me he said, 'Mikey, let me have a look.' When I removed the hanky he looked at me, his face changed from his normal, happy-go-lucky look and he said, 'EOUWW!'

"I said, 'Is it that bad?'

"And he said, 'No, you're going to be fine.'" Mike started laughing, "I felt good because if Ed said I was going to be fine, I was going to be fine. I stopped worrying. When I got to the hospital, I had the best doctor there. Doc A. is what we called him. He was like Ed, he had saved a bunch of people too.

"My bulletproof vest couldn't stop the bullet. It was too large of a caliber. What it did do was spread out the bullet to the size of a quarter. The bullet, part of my uniform shirt, my tee shirt, and my bulletproof vest went into my stomach but didn't penetrate into my intestines.

"When I was in the Intensive Care Unit, a sergeant came to see me. He told me, 'It was just a matter of time. You were taking too many guns off the street. You took what, 30 guns off of the street in eight months? It was inevitable.'

"My uncle, Joseph Charles Rodriguez, called me. 'Mike, you did really good.' That meant more to me than anything. He was a Congressional Medal of Honor recipient from the Korean War. He retired as a colonel from the army. I figured if he complimented me after what he went through, it meant something.

"The guy I shot was trying to become a full-fledged Ontario Black Angel gang member. My first shot had broken his right femur. That's why he started falling. The second round went through his right side, through his chest and lodged near his spine. My third round entered the right side of his neck, nicking his carotid artery then came out of the left side of his neck. He survived. He was on P.C.P. (angel dust). The carload was on its way to a Black Angel party, and the gunman was their protection against any other possible gang hits. He had a minimal record.

"He got seven years for assault with a deadly weapon. The district attorney said they couldn't charge him with attempted murder because he didn't verbalize his intent."

I looked at Mike. If you remember, the suspect said something to him right before he shot him. "Mike, what did the district attorney think the suspect meant when he said, 'That's it fucker!'"

Mike started laughing, "Yeah."

"This bastard was claiming self-defense. He claimed he had his hands up and I shot him three times. Even though he had a gun. So, he had no choice but to shoot me to save his life.

"He was out in four and a quarter-years."

*****

"The shotgun failed because the firing pin was broken. It wouldn't have fired no matter how many times I pulled the trigger."

*****

"Robert, here's the kicker. Ten years later I got a call to go to the station. When I got there, a guy was standing in the lobby. I didn't recognize him. He asked me, 'You don't recognize me do you?'

"I answered, 'No? Why should I? Have we met?'

"He said, 'It's me.' And he gave me his name.

"It was the guy who shot me.

"All the officers came out because they had heard the guy who shot me was in the lobby.

"The guy said to me, 'I need you to talk to my son. I don't want him to become what I became. Can you please talk to him?'

"One of the sergeants who was a real laid-back guy pulled me aside, 'Hey'a, you alright?'

"I answered, 'Yeah, he just wants me to talk to his son.'

"The sergeant said, 'Ain't that fucking weird?'

"I took him and his son to one of the interview rooms. I told him, 'You don't have to head down this path you are heading. What happened between your father and I was in a different time and place, and you don't have to go that way. But if you continue the way you are going, what's going to happen to your kids? Will they be gang members also? What your dad is trying to tell you is it's nothing to be proud of. Don't become a gang member."

Ladies and gentlemen, this is so telling of the magnificent character of this man. If I had been Mike, I would have wanted to kill him.

"You know, Robert, I spent 31 years as an Ontario cop, and I thought it was the ultimate job. But I have six kids. Two of them are two teachers, one is a social clinician, one is a Fontana cop, another is an Army combat medic, and my youngest is a high school freshman. Now, I have four grandchildren and my wife, and I have them five days a week. Robert, I now have the greatest job in the world, being a grandpa."

See, I told you he was a great guy.

*****

Mike Macias received the Ontario Police Department's Bravery Award for his actions on the night of August 25, 1979. This is the second highest award that can be bestowed upon its sworn officers.

Chapter 5

A Hard Lesson

Whittier Blvd. and Clela Ave., Los Angeles, CA

When Allan got to West Hollywood Station Detectives in 1994, I was already thinking of checking out of the department.

Retiring.

I had been a Detective since 1991. My knee was a total wreck, every step was a knife stabbing my knee joint. Having broken it in 1988, it was not getting better.

Allan came on the department at the end of 1981. He prides himself on being an athlete. A baseball player. By 1994 he had already worked patrol, had been a drill instructor at the Los Angeles Sheriff's Academy, and been promoted to sergeant.

Allan has been plagued throughout his career by the comments, "Pretty Boy," "Poster Boy," "Golden Boy," and such. He takes his body seriously. Keeping in shape is all-important to him. He believes cops should be in shape. It is the only way you can efficiently do your job, and at 54 he sports a trim, fit, energetic, muscular figure in his uniform. His blue eyes are clear, his smile huge, and his handshake firm and strong.

The few times I happened to be working out at the West Hollywood Station gym at the same time as him, he would be on the treadmill, shirtless, sweating over rippling deltoids, biceps, and a six-pack. Allan has a quiet self-assurance that gives the impression he believes he is always right. He is so good looking and articulate and self-assured, you get the impression he is infallible. I think because of these traits; some people naturally don't trust him or like him. I feel it is their own lack of self-confidence that is showing through.

Allan is smart. He holds a master's degree he worked hard on for some years while on the department. Let me tell you, he is smart, but at the same time is not afraid to let you know when he doesn't know something. It is something I really appreciated about him. I had been in detectives three years before he arrived. He was not afraid to ask questions and let us know he had things to learn.

He is humble. After promoting to lieutenant, he would go out on patrol as often as possible. This is very uncommon for lieutenants, but he believes it was good for the morale of the troops to see their watch commander, their shift leader, take the rear of a location on a containment during a burglary call.

He is a brave person. Example: Allan was stuck as a lieutenant for many years and seemed he would end his career as such. He believed he was captain material and let it be known he would like to work positions that would round out his experience to that end. He was stymied at every turn. He was told by one very powerful, and high-ranking Sheriff, he was not liked by his troops as a supervisor. He was incredulous. He had never heard this before. So, he sent out a questionnaire to the troops on the premise of conducting a study for class about his qualities and qualifications. He then had the survey takers send them in anonymously to a Ph.D. friend of his to objectively write up the findings. Allan says, and rightly so it takes "balls" to be willing to examine what people really think of you. He is right. I don't think I am that brave. Are you? The report was written up. The long and short of it is, he is now a captain.

He also has a great sense of humor you don't see at first. You have to get over his good looks and beneath his surface to see this. An example of this is when we were at West Hollywood Station together. There is an annual 120-mile relay run that goes from the small desert town of

Baker to Las Vegas. Over a hundred sheriffs, and police stations and different law enforcement agencies participate in the race every year. By now you know I am Mexican, but to me it means nothing. I cannot be offended. Racial jokes about Mexicans don't bother me. I have way more self-confidence than that. If you are black or Asian or white or any other race, it means nothing to me. What is important to me is the person you are inside, your character. But if we are honest all races have traits. One trait of a Mexican man's physique is he has no ass. Now I told you how religious Allan is about his body and being in shape. So, this one-year Allan comes back from the Baker to Vegas run he had participated in. I asked him how his run was.

"Bob, I got my ass kicked." He had this huge grin and was staring at me.

"What do you mean?" I was thinking about our drill instructors and how they used to run backwards up mountains next to us as we struggled just to finish the run. I told you Allan had been a drill instructor.

"Well, Bob, I was on the first leg to run. So, we were all standing around waiting for the race to start. All of us were the rabbits, you know we were going to put our team in front at the beginning of the race so we had a good lead. I am warming up, stretching, sort of bounding around a little to get limbered up. And here comes this Mexican deputy. He has his running shorts on. Bob, he is a little overweight, he had a flat flabby ass. I was sort of relieved I wouldn't have to worry about him. I knew I was in better shape than him and could outrun him. He didn't warm up, didn't stretch, nothing. He just stood there waiting for the race to start. When the race started, I got a good lead and was in front. About a mile into it, I heard someone catching me from behind. Before you know it here comes this same Mexican deputy passing me. The last thing I saw was his flat flabby ass running away from me."

Allan and I were both laughing. He because he had been beat, and I because I was thinking about my own snake ass, which is a back with a hole in it.

It is so cool to see a captain whose eyes light up when he talks about his patrol days 27 years ago. He views patrol, riding around in a radio car as a sacred mission and as a game. That's not to say he doesn't take patrol seriously for he does, but he also sees patrol as a contest. "Bob, I hate to lose, more than I love to win. That means I win most of the time. The bad guys need to go to jail."

"Of course, they do Allan, that's why we joined."

"You know the best day of my life? My proudest day? It was not," and he pointed to his office wall covered with awards from the department, "The day I got any of these awards. It was not the day I promoted to sergeant, lieutenant or captain. It was the day my son got off training in patrol. He is a deputy. On that day I suited up as a lieutenant and worked patrol with him for one shift." He was absolutely beaming.

"What kind of deputy is he?"

"I hear stories. It scares me, Bob, because what I hear reminds me of me when I worked patrol. I loved to work, look for bad people. It scares me because it means you are exposing yourself to danger. Now I know how my wife felt. He's already been in a shooting. It was a guy with an AK-47. My son shot him. It scared the hell out of me. I now realize how my wife must have felt with me out in patrol. Sometimes I am amazed when I look and I see my wife still by my side after all these years." I saw the admiration in his eyes he felt for her and for his son. "It is something to remember, your little boy running around with plastic toy guns saying he was going to be a deputy and then actually seeing him as one."

Having grown boys about the same age as Allan's, I could easily understand his feelings. "I never knew you when you worked patrol. In fact, when you came to West Hollywood I was already working detectives."

"I worked East Los Angeles Station. After getting off training, I opted to work the overlap shift."

This is the shift typically from seven p.m. through three a.m. It's a very busy shift.

"My partner Raul and I got abused by dispatch. It's what I wanted. We caught all the hot calls from p.m. shift" (this is the 3 pm to 11pm shift), "so they could get off on time. Then things started heating up on the early morning shift after eleven, and everyone was busy. I loved it. I wouldn't trade those days for anything in the world."

I understood. You get to prove to yourself who you really are out there. You get to know yourself well, and there are no questions about your abilities. No self-doubt. It's hard work; you can get unbelievably over your head busy, but when you handle it all you become a self-assured, confident person.

"A good day for me in those days was a day I worked out before my shift. Then went 10-8 (on duty), ate, took people to jail, then ate again." Allan had a huge grin on his face. "Raul and I ate twice a shift. We were all about handling our calls, taking people to jail, doing the lords work, working out, being in shape."

"It sounds like you knew Raul well."

"Yeah, we were in the academy together, but I didn't know him well then. It was after we got to East L.A. where we worked together and partnered up I got to know him. By May 9, 1986, we were in a groove. We had our routine down. We knew how each other thought and worked well together. We had an informant. I can't remember if he called the station or told us in person about a guy selling P.C.P. in the alley north of Whittier Boulevard at Clela Ave. We were in a marked black and white radio car, but wanted to get this guy. It was about eleven fifteen at night. So, what we did is park south of Whittier in the alley and looked north through some buildings, across Whittier to the alley north of Whittier. Over a little period of time, we saw people drive up to the alley. They would briefly meet some guy who would then leave. Several minutes later the same guy would come back. Some sort of physical exchange would occur, and then the car would drive off. This was going on in the alley north of Whittier at Vancouver, just a block east of Clela."

"A dope deal. Sherm sticks." I said.

"Exactly. We used to call them cools. The Mexicans would dip "Cool" cigarettes in P.C.P. and smoke them. Sherman cigarettes, or Sherms, were mainly used in the black areas. We knew what was going on. The guy would meet a buyer, then leave. He would dip a Cool cigarette in a bottle of liquid P.C.P. then come back and make the money exchange for the P.C.P. cigarette. Anyway, after a few of these exchanges, we decided to grab whomever we could at the alley, see who had drugs and make some arrests. We drove to the alley. When we got there, eight to ten people were standing around. We detained them all. That's when I saw one guy standing off to the side. He was north of the alley on Vancouver, urinating in the front yard of some duplex's bushes."

"Weird?"

"Yeah, we were in a black and white, and this guy was standing not too far away from us just urinating. He was totally ignoring us. I walked over to him and noticed the blank stare. As I got closer I smelled it, the P.C.P. I looked at the back of his pants and could see the outline of what looked like a pack of cigarettes. I gingerly pulled them out while he was urinating and the smell hit me strongly. Whew, P.C.P. It was a pack of Cool cigarettes."

As Allan told this, he pushed his arms away from him, extending them outward pushing his palms forward with his fingers pulled upward. He simultaneously pulled his head backward and to the side away from his arms. It was apparent he was reliving the moment of the strong, ether-like smell of P.C.P.

"I waited until he finished urinating. I then asked him to put his hands behind his back. You know how P.C.P. suspects are, Bob."

"I do." Now I was reliving some of my nasty experiences with P.C.P. users. P.C.P. does strange things to people. If they are in an okay mood, kind'a mellow, you want to keep them like that. Because if you don't, you will have the fight of your life on your hands.

"I was doing everything to keep things low key. He complied. As soon as I got him handcuffed, I walked him to the radio car and put him in the backseat. He was cool. Compliant. You have to understand we had a lot going on. Raul was watching ten guys. Ten guys who were probably buying or who had bought P.C.P. Some of them might have been under the influence of P.C.P. So, while I was arresting the one guy, my mind was also on Raul and with half my vision focused on him. You know ten people are a lot to control."

"Absolutely, Allan. Your hands were full."

"So now I had the one guy arrested. We dealt with the ten guys and found nothing. We cut them loose and went into the alley to look for the P.C.P. bottle the one guy was dipping the cigarettes into then selling. We looked in clumps of grass, under rocks, drainpipes, you know the usual, but we couldn't find it. We decided to drive a block away in the alley and hang out to see if the guy selling the P.C.P. would come back to get his bottle. The guy was in the backseat and was moving around. Raul and I kept telling him, 'Stop moving around, the handcuffs are going to get real tight.' He kept moving around. Fidgeting around a lot. Pretty unusual in retrospect, but we were focused on getting the guy selling the P.C.P. After five or ten minutes we drove back to Vancouver Ave., had a quick look-see to see if anyone was hanging around waiting for us to leave. We didn't see anyone. We decided to go to the station to book our suspect.

"We swung around to northbound Clela. We were in the 700 block when I heard firecrackers. I was driving and I heard the firecrackers. Things slowed down, time slowed, instantly. I thought, 'Who the fuck is throwing firecrackers at our car? Why would anyone be throwing firecrackers at our car?' Then I realized the firecrackers were loud, coming right from my right ear. 'No, no one is throwing firecrackers at our car,' I realized, 'the guy in the backseat has firecrackers. Why the fuck is the guy in the backseat lighting firecrackers?'"

"Wow," I said.

Allan laughed, "Bob, all those thoughts went through my head as quickly as it took for the guy to fire off three rounds in rapid succession. It was three quick pops, firecracker pops that took forever to complete. Time was really slow now."

"Gunfire!"

"Yep. The guy, the suspect was little. About a 120-pound little Mexican guy. He was standing with his head crouched down against the roof firing at me with his hands handcuffed behind his back from the back seat. I said to myself, '**FUCK NO!** This guy's got a gun. How does this guy have a gun?' I was incredulous. I couldn't understand how this was happening because I couldn't understand how the guy had a gun. The rational side of my thinking was realizing and understanding he had a gun. But because I couldn't figure out how, I was having trouble believing it was true. But it was happening. While my brain was trying to process this, I was still getting shot at. All this was really happening in milliseconds, but felt like it was taking hours to transpire."

"Allan, were you scared?'

"No, Bob. It sounds like I should have been, but I was so busy trying to figure out what was going on I didn't have time to be scared. I thought, 'We got to get out of the kill zone.' I went to put the car in park so we could get out. And I remember, just like I'm sitting here with you right now, the grinding. It wouldn't get into park because we were still moving forward. We were probably going about ten miles an hour or so, and the car would not go into park. It was just grinding the gears. I opened the car door and bailed."

"With the car moving?"

"Yep. What's amazing is Raul bailed with me. At the same time. I told you we were tuned into each other perfectly. We were probably going about ten miles an hour. When I bailed out of the car, I was moving my legs as fast as I could. I didn't fall. Neither did Raul. We just ran with the momentum of the moving radio car. When we stopped we were about ten feet apart. We turned toward the radio car. He was on the right, and I was on the left. I kept thinking, 'How in the fuck did this guy get a gun?' When I told you the guy was in the back seat standing, firing at me, I had not really seen him doing it as much as I felt him doing it. It had to be that way because the firecrackers were going off right next to my right ear. It was amazing, Bob. I should be dead."

I looked at Allan. I understood perfectly.

"My partner and I cleared leather (a term for getting your gun out of its holster). I drew down (aimed his gun at) on my radio car. That was the weirdest part. Drawing down on my own radio car. To me that was surreal. The car crashed into some parked cars. I still had the thought going through my head, almost like a little doubt, 'Does he really have a gun?' I looked at my partner. He looked at me. Weird we looked at each other at the same exact time. We smiled at each other and nod-ded." Allan laughed, "It's like we both acknowledged to each other the guy had a gun and gave each other permission in a way. Like, 'Do you see it like I see it?' We opened fire. Opened fire on our own radio car."

Allan had that look on his face, which told me shooting at your radio car is not a normal thing. "How many rounds did you fire?"

"Four, we each fired four rounds."

"Time returned to normal now. I can't tell you how long it took for all this to happen. I was now behind cover, behind a car on the left side of the street. My arm, my right triceps hurt like hell. It was burning. I felt liquid, hot burning liquid on my arm. I was still drawn down on my car. Something was telling me I'd been shot. My mind was still in disbelief. When you're shot, you expect to see someone shooting at you. I never saw that. I just heard the firecrackers. I yelled to Raul to get help. Remember we were behind the radio car and did not know if the suspect was still ready and able to shoot us. He was bouncing off the inside of the car."

"Allan, why didn't you keep shooting? You were justified."

"I know, Bob. Homicide later asked us the same question. My only answer I have is that I felt the immediate threat was over. He was still handcuffed. There was still a threat, but I felt there was time to shoot if we had to."

Not for the first time since writing this book did my respect go up for another colleague. He once again proved we are not assassins, not predatory animals looking for revenge, or looking to kill someone. He was in control of an uncontrollable situation.

"Bob, these were in the days when we had no handheld radios. The only help was to go and knock on someone's door. Raul couldn't go to the radio car to call on our radio for help; the suspect was inside the car with a gun. I saw him run to a neighbor's door. The suspect was really bouncing around in the back seat. He was absolutely wild. Like a caged animal. Just going crazy. He was bouncing off the windows, off the back screen, off the doors, going nuts, screaming. The radio car was shaking. My arm was killing me now. I was focused on the radio car; Raul had run to a house and was presumably knocking on someone's door to get help. Then I saw the suspect with his back against the screen, with his back against the front seats, somehow raise up both feet and start kicking the rear window of the radio car. This was not going well. The unbelievable force of his kicks was amazing. He was just a little guy, but he was so strong it was unfathomable. I yelled at the top of my lungs, 'Raul come back!'"

"Why Allan, why'd you do that?"

"I knew from the force of his kicks he was going to kick out the rear window. Just as I caught a glimpse of my partner running back, the window literally exploded. Obliterated. Shattered glass fragments flew everywhere. He was climbing out of the rear window. I thought, 'No way is this guy getting away.' He came out of the window headfirst. I ran to the back of the radio car and got to him as he was clearing the trunk. As I was grabbing him and throwing him to the ground, I saw Raul with his baton out heading straight for us. As he was raising the baton to hit him, I thought, 'Please don't; you're going to hit me.' I now had the suspect on the ground. I was lying on top of him, hugging him on the ground, wrapped up. Lying in the shattered glass. 'Go get help,' I yelled. Now that our unit was clear he ran to the radio and put out a call for help. As I was on top of the suspect, I peeled his fingers open, and there was a little .25 caliber Raven semi-automatic."

"What did you think when you saw the gun?"

"It just confirmed what I had all along failed to fully comprehend. He had a gun."

"And the backup units?"

"Man, it felt so good to hear the sirens," then Allan laughed, "then it felt so bad."

"Why?"

"I heard them coming. Closer and closer they were coming, then at the apex, the sound faded further away. They passed us. Raul had given out the wrong street. I had a little discussion with my partner, right there while we were lying on the street hugging the suspect, as to where we were. We didn't agree. Finally, I yelled out at the top of my lungs, 'WHERE ARE WE? WHERE ARE WE?' I heard a little voice come from the inside of a house, 'Clela.' We put out the right address and help found us."

"Bob, my arm was really hurting by then. Really, really sore. They were going to send me to some hospital, but the lieutenant showed up and said, 'Take him to Los Angeles County Medical Center, it's one of the best trauma centers in the world!' So off I went to L.C.M.C. When I got to the hospital, they were so full they put me in the hallway. They had taken my gun belt away from me. So here I was in the hallway, in uniform, and with no gun. I was alone. I had no one guarding me. No gun, no cops!"

"Allan, all the gang members go there after they get shot up."

"I know, and their friends. The sergeant got there shortly after I arrived and just blew a gasket."

I smiled and shook my head. Such seemingly simple things get overlooked in critical incidents.

"Okay, Bob. I was in the best trauma unit in the world. Where multitudes of gunshot victims go every year, and they miss the bullet."

"What?"

"Yeah. The bullet went in just above my right elbow and zipped up the back of my arm to the upper triceps. When they x-rayed me, it was from the elbow to my forearm. Well below the triceps. The reason? Because I had a cut on my forearm. The cut was from the glass when I was lying on the ground with the suspect. The hospital assumed it was an exit wound. That was even after I told them the pain I had was in my upper triceps. They said the bullet exited my forearm, the x-rays showed no bullets in my body, and they sent me home."

"Oh my God."

"Yep. It wasn't until several days later when my arm blew up I went back. They x-rayed my triceps and found the bullet. They gave me a local anesthetic and took it out. Here's what's scary. I later saw the radio car. There were bullet holes in the windshield. All the bullet holes were patterned in the area in front of where my head should have been. If I had ever looked to my right, to see what was going on in the back seat once I heard the firecrackers, I don't think we would be having this conversation. If he wasn't so whacked on P.C.P. I'd be dead. I'd be dead. I should be dead.

"Bob, I got an apology letter from the suspect before we went to court. I tore it up and threw it away. What a bunch of bull. He had tried to kill me, then say he was sorry.

"It was weird when I got back in a radio car after the shooting. When I made my first arrest, I couldn't take my eyes off of this guy in the back seat. I kept looking at him to make sure he didn't have a gun."

"Allan, did you ever figure it out? How he got the gun?"

"Yeah. Sometimes I'll hear they taught my shooting at the academy or at an advanced officer training class and it's all about proper searching techniques. What techniques can they learn from my shooting? There was no technique! Because there was no search! Bob, I never searched the guy. I handcuffed him and put him in the backseat of the radio car. Remember I told you my partner was watching ten guys, and how I was watching my partner, as well as the suspect? I was focused on keeping the guy cool. He was on P.C.P. I wanted to keep him calm. I missed one of the most…the most important steps. I never searched the guy."

*****

The suspect was a gang member. He received eight years. He was out in four, despite being convicted of attempted murder on a peace officer.

Chapter 6
The Will to Survive

Brannick Ave. and Floral Drive, Los Angeles, CA

It was the winter of 2011. I'd heard about the incident the day after it happened. A deputy from the East Los Angeles County Sheriff's Patrol Station had been shot.

Irma stopped me as I was going to my office. Irma is a very pretty, and talkative support staff for our investigative bureau. "Did you hear about the shooting?"

"Yes, Irma," I replied.

Knowing I was retired from the Sheriff's Department she asked me, "Do you know Danny Reyes?"

"No, I don't know him, did he get shot?"

"No, his partner did. You know my sister is married to Danny's brother. We see him at family gatherings."

Irma described the incident as she knew it. It chilled me to the bone. "Irma, tell Danny from one deputy sheriff to another, I'm proud of him and he did a great job. I'm glad he's alive."

*****

When I started this book, I decided I wanted to talk to Danny about the incident. I got his number from Irma.

When I talked to Danny, I immediately liked him, just like you would if you met him. He is a real gentleman, soft-spoken, humble, and honest. I told him about this book, and he was interested in talking.

After meeting Danny I liked him even more. Over the course of the next four hours I not only came to like this man, but to respect his courage of steel.

*****

Danny is a fairly non-descript man. Not too tall. He is a quiet person. "Robert, when people meet me they can't believe I'm a cop. I am the youngest of eleven children. I grew up just a little north and east of downtown Los Angeles. My dad demanded us children be respectful toward others and always behave. He taught us to be giving to other people. All eleven of us went in the right direction. None of us got into trouble. We went to church every Sunday. I am normally quiet in a crowd and shy. I am better one on one."

Danny joined the Los Angeles County Sheriff's Department in 1990. I asked him what he thought of the Academy.

"Robert, I thought it was tough. I went in blind. I had no idea what to expect. I lost 25 pounds, but it prepared me. I now know the really tough training I received prepared me. I was really proud I made it. So many in our class dropped out. They couldn't make it."

"Danny why Los Angeles County? Why not the Los Angeles Police Department? You lived and grew up in an L.A.P.D. area."

He smiled. "I was taught by my dad that cops should be respected. I got a little bit of a bad taste in my mouth with L.A.P.D. when I was younger. I was a good kid. I was not a gang member. I never got in trouble. I was responsible and respectful toward others. When I was going to college, I must have been about 19 years old, I got pulled over by two L.A.P.D. officers. It was a female and a male officer. The female officer told me I had a taillight out. She got me out of the car and walked me to the back of my car. She was right, my tail light was out. I tapped the light and it came on. She got angry with me as if I had done something wrong. She pointed and told me to go and stand on the sidewalk. She really shook me up. I didn't know what I had done wrong, and I was feeling bad, really bad inside about the encounter. I must have had a scared look on my face because the male officer who was at the sidewalk told me not to worry about it, that they weren't going to cite me. The next thing I knew she wrote me a ticket for a broken taillight. I was taking criminal justice classes at college. I vowed if I ever became a cop, I would treat all people with respect. Every day when I go to work, I try my best to treat people well and leave them with a good feeling about cops. I want to help people if I can. I mean that's why I joined."

He told me more about himself. He first went to patrol at Pico Rivera Sheriff's Station. He always wanted to work at East Los Angeles Station though, and three years later, in 1999, he transferred there. Danny got a reputation as a hardworking deputy. While working day shift, some of the other deputies told him to slow down because he was making them look bad. In 2001, he was promoted to the position of field training officer. For the next ten years he trained over 20 different new patrol deputies. For you non-cops, this is no small feat. Every time you get a new field deputy, you have to take them from point A to Z. You are responsible for them to eventually be able to function alone in a radio car (police car). There is a lot for the trainee to absorb and a lot for the training officer to impart.

"Robert, I am patient," Danny said, "They gave me a lot of the trainees that had problems. I am not only patient; I am very fair. I wanted to help them learn if they put forth the effort. If they couldn't make it off training with me, they couldn't make it with anyone. In January 2011, I had a trainee. He had been with me five weeks."

Danny was 44 years old at the time. To be 44 years old in a radio car is tough: The task of manning a radio car on a daily basis is strenuous for a young person, much less a man of 44 years. It is just a fact the older you get, the more you break down. This is especially true when you are getting in and out of a radio car carrying around forty pounds of gear all day (yes, when you add up the guns, ammo, boots, handcuffs, etc. it can add up to 40 pounds). Add to that the foot pursuits, fights, and high stress, and you can see the reality is that patrol is for young people.

"Robert, you know that East Los Angeles has a lot of hills. I was beginning to notice that as I was walking up and down stairs and hills, I would get a little short of breath. I had always prided myself on being in shape. You and I know if you are working patrol, you have to be in shape. So I usually worked out, but around that time I had slacked off a little. I got back into working out. The morning of January 11, 2011 I went to the gym. My shift started at 2 p.m., but I got busy and didn't have time to eat before my shift. I thought I would eat once I got to the station, at the beginning of my shift."

He looked at me. He had a smile that was sly. And I knew why.

"Danny, you didn't eat did you? You had a few calls stacked up didn't you?"

"Yeah Robert, we had calls waiting as soon as our shift started and I couldn't eat. Then I had a parolee at large run from me."

A "parolee at large" is a person who is on parole and wanted for arrest by the parole board.

"We set up a containment for the parolee, and that lasted a couple of hours. Before I knew it, it was seven p.m. and I still hadn't eaten. I had a headache and was lightheaded. I told my trainee we were going to the station to eat. Remember I had worked out that morning, so I was really running low on energy."

I was looking at Danny. I guess I had that look. "Robert, I know. I should have just gone back to the station."

I shrugged my shoulders and smiled, "It's hard isn't it? You're out on the streets, sniffing around. Then you see something out of place. It's like a dog. You have to see what's going on. You have to put your nose in it."

"Exactly. It's what we do. As I was going back to the station, I saw a car parked at Floral Drive and Brannick Ave. There was something wrong. The car was parked in the red zone in front of a bus stop on Brannick."

He described the scene. It was seven p.m. January 11, 2011, a cold and windy Tuesday evening. The sun had set and it was dark. A woman was sitting in the driver's seat of a white car. She was parked on the west side of Brannick Ave. facing south at Floral Drive. She was parked in the red zone. Behind the bus stop was a chain-link fence. Just south of the chain-link fence is a house Danny knew. He knew the house because it was a drug house. Numerous arrests had been made there.

"Robert, I knew the family that lived at the drug house. I had arrested some family members from the house in the past. Narcotics had conducted raids of the house in the past. But the thing is we got along. They knew me. I had always been fair with them. I was always respectful to them. I never roughed anyone up. I always explained the way things were and they seemed to respect me. When I would drive by the house, if they were outside, they would wave hello to me. I would wave back."

This seemed so typical of the man I had just met. A gentleman who quietly went about his business, making the streets safer in a gentlemanly way.

"I thought to myself they must be there to score drugs from the drug house. I crept up next to the side of the car." Danny put his hands side by side demonstrating to me his position that night. "So, my radio car's passenger door was just a little behind the woman's driver's door. I told my trainee to talk to her, and find out what was going on."

Danny got that little look in his eye which told me, "Wait there's more."

"As my trainee was speaking to the woman, I crept up just a little more and looked past her into the passenger seat. That's when I saw him. A passenger was slouched down and was totally ignoring that we were there. He was sitting, staring straight ahead without moving. He was wearing a beanie and a heavy corduroy jacket."

"Weird, huh?" I said to Danny.

"Yeah really weird. I knew something was wrong. You know the feeling."

"Oh yeah Danny, I know."

"The woman was telling my trainee she stopped to adjust her knee brace. The guy was just sitting there staring forward, ignoring us, not interested in the fact two cops were talking to them. Weird."

"What did you do?"

"I didn't know the guy. I told my trainee to get out of the car and talk to the woman. I got out and walked around the front of the car to the sidewalk to talk to the passenger. When I got there, I recognized him. He was a gang member I had talked to before. I knew him and I knew he was on parole. He was no longer stone still. He was fidgeting around now, but he still was not looking at me. He had a Dr. Pepper in his hands, and I told him to put it down. After I recognized him, I knew I was going to get him out of the car, and I wanted him to get rid of the soda. When he placed the Dr. Pepper on the center console, it tipped sideways and started spilling out into the car. Any normal person would pick it up, straighten it up, right? I mean it was a nice car, clean you know? But he just let it continue to spill out. Again, it was weird; it was as if he could not pay attention to what he was doing. After putting the soda can down, he was now fidgety. His hands kept going toward the inside of his jacket, toward his waistband. I kept telling him, 'Keep your hands where I can see them.' He was jittery, like he was trying to subdue his hyperactivity but just couldn't control himself. I was on edge now. Nothing was fitting into place. Nothing was normal about the situation. I kept looking at his hands to make sure he wasn't going for a gun. But he was still in the car. I wanted him out."

I was on edge now. Looking and listening to Danny, I understood the gravity of the situation. In situations like this you really don't know what you got, but you know something is not right. He knew he had a parolee in the car and the parolee was on the edge of not listening to his orders. It's scary because there is something in the air that is not right. You cannot go to court and say, "The air changed," or that "Things felt different." People will not understand. They'll look at you like you're nuts, but the air does change, things do feel different. When you are in those situations the change from normalcy to "oh shit" is palpable.

"Robert, I opened the door, and he knew exactly what he was going to do. He hid the front of his body when he got out. What he did was step out with his right foot, then pivoted to his left, so the front of his body was always facing the car and out of my sight. He then slammed his left shoulder into the front of my body. This knocked me back about three feet. He then took off running south on Brannick on the sidewalk.

"Remember I had a parolee at large run away from me at the beginning of the shift? Well, I was not about to let another guy get away from me. I chased him and caught him about five feet away. I tackled him from behind. Down we both went to the sidewalk. And just like that the fight was on. At the time I had no idea where my trainee was. I later learned he was sitting inside the radio car running the woman's driver license."

"Danny, what do you mean the fight was on?"

"He was so strong. I couldn't control him. I was trying to get his hands so I could handcuff him and he was elbowing me, I was elbowing him. He was kneeing me and I was kneeing him, as hard as I could. I was punching him. It seemed he felt no pain. He didn't get tired. Up to this point, he had not said a word. Nothing. We were rolling on the sidewalk. First, I was on top, and then he was on top, then me again. One time when he was on top I felt a hard tug on my gun. I knew he was trying to take my weapon. It was terrifying. I was terrified; he was trying to get my gun to kill me. And I couldn't stop him. He was so strong. Overwhelmingly so. We kept fighting, desperately. Searching for some advantage, some edge. He was so strong I couldn't comprehend it. It was like he was superhuman. Nothing I did affected him. And he still had not said a word. I could not get the upper hand. He would not stop. I couldn't stop him."

As Danny was telling me this, I got it. Folks, I understood. Been there, done that. I'd fought dusters before. Guys on P.C.P., phencyclidine (known as angel dust). They feel no pain. They don't say a word. You can't hurt them. P.C.P. was used as a large game animal tranquilizer. You know, for lions, tigers, and bears. As Danny was telling me the story, I was thinking he was fighting a "duster."

"That's when I looked up and saw my partner coming. We made eye contact. I'd never been so glad to see someone in my life. I was so tired, exhausted is more like it. We'd only been fighting for about a minute, but it felt like ten minutes. The woman was screaming, 'NO, NO, PLEASE STOP, PLEASE STOP, NO!' The suspect then did something I couldn't believe. He stood up. He stood up with me on his back. How he did it, I could not understand. I was so exhausted, and he stood up like nothing. Like I wasn't there. As he stood up facing my trainee, he said, "What the FUCK?"

"Danny, he finally spoke?"

"Yep he did. Robert, I couldn't see his face, and now I couldn't see my trainee either, but I was thinking maybe we can get this guy under control. My partner is here and he's going to give up. You know, now it was two on one and he's going to give up. Robert, understand everything was happening in fractions of a second. That's when I heard it, the firecracker. I thought, 'What was that? A firecracker? Where did that come from?' I could not see my partner. Robert, we're talking milliseconds here, things are happening very, very, fast. The woman is still screaming, pleading plaintively crying out, 'NO, PLEASE STOP, NO, NO!!!' The suspect turned to his left so very fast, faster than you could believe, and I was face to face with the barrel of a gun. Instinctively I reached out and grabbed the barrel. It was a pistol. Up to this point, time was normal. Now things slowed down, very, very, slowly. He slowly shoved the barrel of the gun toward me. I pushed it away. I was slowly thinking, 'I've... got... to... get... the... barrel... of... the... gun... out... of ... my... face. What... if ... the... gun... goes... off?' Each shove he made and each shove I made back was no longer milliseconds, but felt like minutes. I was so tired. I tried to turn the barrel away from my face. His hands, his arms were steel. Steel. I could not budge the barrel. I was using all my strength, all my force, and I could not turn the barrel from my face. Fighting for what seemed like an hour, trying to control the barrel, and get it away from me, but in reality the fight was another two and a half minutes. I had been fighting the suspect now for three and a half minutes."

"Danny, you were tired going into this. You had worked out, you hadn't eaten, you were lightheaded, and you had a headache from not eating."

"Robert, I had been fighting all out for three and a half minutes. I was so tired. The only time I've been that tired was when I was in the academy. I knew my partner had been shot although I hadn't seen him yet and still did not know where he was."

Folks, if you think this is easy, I invite you to put on some boxing gloves and go hit and knee a heavy bag non-stop for three and a half minutes. Make sure you worked out that morning and make sure it's seven p.m. Oh and make sure you don't eat all day. Also, make sure you don't stop punching and kneeing that heavy bag for one second. Now imagine while you are doing this someone is trying to kill you, and you'll understand what Danny was going through.

"That's when I gave up. Robert, I gave up. I couldn't fight anymore. I was so exhausted and in such physical pain, so physically exhausted, I couldn't do it anymore. When I gave up, time stopped. Actually stopped. I was in a dream. It wasn't real. I was in shock this was happening. I still had the barrel of the gun in my hands, but I was no longer pushing the gun away, and he was no longer shoving the gun at me. I just didn't want to have to have the pain anymore, the exhaustion. He had beat me. I was beyond nausea, beyond out of breath. I was too fatigued to go on. I accepted that getting shot and dying would be easier than the pain I felt by fighting. I accepted it. I accepted my death."

We were silent for a while, Danny and I.

"Danny, what happened next?" I prompted.

He looked at me. He answered softly. "My family. They were behind me. I could see them. Although I was facing the suspect, I could see my family behind me. They were above my head. I could hear them inside my head, my wife, my kids, and my parents. They were watching me dispassionately, but they were talking to me. 'Don't give up! Fight back! Fight, fight!' I don't know where it came from. I thought I was done. But I got really, really angry. I believe the word is enraged. Unbelievable rage. I didn't know I could get that angry. To actually want to kill another human. I said to myself, 'FUCK YOU! I'm not going to let you kill me. I'm not going to die. I'm NOT GOING TO LET YOU KILL ME!!!' Time went back to normal. No more stopped or slow-motion time."

I smiled. I understood what he meant. Danny had had enough. The umbrage that a lowlife like this was going to deprive him of his life. To let this nothing, this less than human scum, deprive his family of his love was too much to accept.

"With all my strength, thinking I was going to rip the gun out of his hands, I pulled to my left and shoved. He still held onto the gun. I spun him 180 degrees. I had pulled his whole body around. His back was now up against the chain-link fence. With every fiber of my soul, I turned the gun away from my face. This was the first time in three minutes I was not facing the gun. With another burst of energy, I twisted the gun in his hands moving the barrel away from my face. The gun was now at a 90-degree angle facing to my right. I let go of the gun with my right hand, while still holding onto the gun with my left hand. I did this so I could draw my gun. I was thinking I was going to unload all 16 bullets into him. Robert, I knew if I didn't kill this fucker, he was going to kill me. I fully intended to put all my bullets into him. When I let go of the gun with my right hand, he fired the gun twice. Both shots were simultaneous, almost like one shot."

My face went blank, and I think I blanched when Danny told me this. "Danny, why hadn't the gun fired before? It should have fired. You were still holding the gun by the barrel. Nothing had changed except that you were now holding the gun barrel with one hand instead of two."

"I know Robert. I don't have an answer for that. I can't figure it out either. When he fired the gun though, my hand stove piped the gun. I didn't know I had stove piped the gun at the time though."

I was incredulous. I could not understand why the gun had not fired during the three minutes before while Danny was fighting over the gun. Stovepiping is when a shell does not fully eject from the gun after being fired, and now the gun is jammed and will not fire again.

"Robert, as soon as I let go of the gun with my right hand I drew my gun. It was a smooth pull, a clean draw. I drew very fast, it was my last chance. Right after he fired, I laid my gun over my left hand, laid it right on top of the suspect's gun. I remember, Robert, that's when the suspect gave up. I don't mean he said anything, like, 'I give up.' What I mean is his body sort of stopped fighting. He went a little limp; his arms went limp for just a millisecond before I shot him two times in the face, in the mouth. He knew at the end I had won."

"His body language?"

"Yes, his body language. I meant to shoot him in the face. I knew I had to stop him and in my mind, the only way to immediately stop him was to shoot him in the face. I was just trying to stop him from fighting so I wouldn't die. I backed up still covering him with my gun. He was hanging on the fence. His corduroy jacket had hung up on the fence, and he was hanging there completely limp with his shoulders pulled up. His beanie had fallen off his head, and his hair was down over his face. I couldn't see his face at all, and I didn't know where I had shot him. I only knew he wasn't moving and the gun was no longer in his hand. There was no blood."

"Danny, I thought you were going to empty all 16 bullets into him."

"Robert, when I shot him twice, which happened so quickly it was again just like one shot, he went limp. The threat was over. I had no need to keep shooting him."

My admiration for Danny just went up 100-fold. He was not an animal, like the man he was fighting. He was not fighting to kill someone. He was fighting to survive. There is a difference. Even after all he had gone through just seconds ago, but now a lifetime ago, he still held on to his principles. He still believed in doing the right thing, and he acted honorably.

"I kept backing up covering the suspect with my gun, and then looked back. My trainee was standing, leaning against the radio car. His hand was covering the right side of his face. He looked at me, moved his hand and said, 'I'm sorry.' I could see where the bullet was bulging, trying to come out of his right cheekbone through the side of his face. I told him there was nothing to be sorry for. He was alive, and everything was going to be okay. There was a trickle of blood on his left cheekbone where the bullet had entered. I looked down on the sidewalk. There were two guns there. One was the gun I had fought the suspect over, and the other was a revolver that didn't belong to my partner or myself. I later found out the suspect had had two guns in his waistband."

"Danny, that's why he kept going toward his waistband while he was sitting in the car."

"Yes, Robert. I believe he wanted to kill me from the beginning. The woman later told the homicide investigators when I pulled the radio car beside their car, the suspect said he was not going back to prison."

"I got my handheld radio and transmitted I needed assistance. That my partner was shot. Nothing, no response. I then looked at my radio and found the frequencies had become all mixed up during the fight. I tried to reset the radio to the correct frequencies, but my fingers would no longer obey me. My hands and fingers were shaking. I got in the radio car and put out the call. I waited and waited for the deputies to come and help me. No response. Finally, I heard the deputies on the radio asking where I was. The radio dispatch had misheard my location; they sent cars to Floral and Mednik. I had to repeat my location four more times before they understood me."

"And your partner, your trainee?"

"Oh, interesting that before help arrived, the family in the drug house came out with towels and helped my trainee. They put the towels on his now bleeding bullet wound. He had taken a 40-millimeter bullet to his right cheek. The bullet traveled under his nose to the other side of his face. He ended up losing an eye. His jaw was also broken."

"My trainee went to the hospital. I went to the hospital. While in the emergency room I saw through open curtains nurses and doctors doing chest compressions on someone. I immediately thought it was my trainee and I lost my composure. I found out they were doing compressions on the suspect I had shot. Try as the doctors did, they could not save his life."

I looked at Danny, "Who was this guy? This guy who wanted to kill you?"

"He was a gangbanger. He had been arrested over 20 times. Robert when they tested his blood, they found P.C.P., cocaine, methamphetamine, alcohol, and marijuana in his system. He had just finished up a seven-year prison sentence. The woman was just an acquaintance. She was not a criminal. I think she was just giving him a ride somewhere. She saw the suspect pull the gun and shoot my trainee in the face.

"At the hospital, my trainee's family came up to me one by one and thanked me for saving his life. His mother thanked me for saving her son's life.

"I was pretty banged up, but the worst was my right thigh. I think when the suspect and I were rolling around on the sidewalk and as I was kneeing him I hit his revolver with my right thigh. It might have saved my life because the best I can figure is when I kneed him, I knocked the revolver out of his waistband.

"At the suspect's funeral there was a rumor circulating that some family members wanted to have me killed for what I had done. After going back out on the streets on patrol, I was approached by a member from another gang. He told me it was a good thing I killed the suspect. I asked him why. He said the guy was out of control. He had been walking around with two guns in his waistband and waving them around. He was always doped up and threatening people. The gang member told me it was just a matter of time before he killed someone. The suspect just didn't care about anyone or anything. He thanked me for what I did. Interesting, huh?"

"Danny, are you a hero?"

"No, I'm not, Robert. As a law enforcement officer it is part of my job. I see it as an incident I was involved in."

"What are you proud of Danny?'

"Robert, I've tried to help so many kids stay away from gangs. I mean I grew up not too far from East Los Angeles. I didn't understand why, why kids would want to live their life that way. I've seen them go from normal kids to associating with gangs. I would find them on the streets at midnight, carrying guns. Kids, 12-year-old kids, with guns and 40-ounce beer bottles or weed. I'd send them to juvenile hall. They then got out at 18 as adults only to go to County Jail then to State Prison. When they come out, they are on parole. Some I have known have been killed. Others are in and out of prison. I once got a call from some parents because they were having a hard time with their 12-year-old boy. He was a gang member and his parents could not control him. I asked him why he wanted to be a part of it. Do you know what he told me?"

I looked at Danny's eyes, and I saw the pain.

"The kid started crying and told me, 'What else am I going to do?'"

*****

Danny is a peer counselor for other deputies who have gone through critical incidents. He also lectures at the Los Angeles County Sheriff's Academy to new recruits on officer survival and safety. He is a person who is all about giving back and helping as much as he can.

*****

Danny Reyes received the "Medal of Valor" from the Los Angeles County Sheriff's Department for his actions on the evening of January 11, 2011. This is the highest award that can be given.

In 2008, Congress created the Congressional Badge of Bravery. It is awarded once a year to those in law enforcement who have performed an act characterized as bravery. Danny Reyes was the recipient of this award on April 1, 2014. He is the first Deputy from the Los Angeles County Sheriff's Department to receive this award.

Chapter 7

Ex Von der Schimmel-Schultz Heide

Banyan St. and Caldwell St., Ontario, CA

Shortly after I finished writing chapter one, I let Ernie read my story.

He finished and looked at me. Not a word. Not one word did he utter. This is uncharacteristic of him.

About five seconds went by. "Well?" I asked.

Holding the stapled manuscript, he lightly threw his arms up and to the side, but still said nothing. His face was changed now that he had finished.

Ten seconds went by. Again, I asked him, "Well?'

"Well what?" he said.

"Well, what did you think?"

"It's good," he said without much enthusiasm.

His face was deadpan, and some of the color had drained from it. He was not his usual self. Then I noticed the rims of his eyes had turned red.

I pressed him. "Ernesto, what do you really think? Were you there when you read the story? Could you feel the intensity?"

"Robert, you took me back to my... my incident."

"What incident?" I asked.

"It ruined my first marriage."

"What did?"

"The shooting."

Now it was my turn to be silent. I looked at him, but he was no longer meeting my eyes. An embarrassed silence passed between us. "Ernie," I finally said, this silence so unnatural between us, "what shooting?"

"I still have him," he answered.

"Who?"

He ignored my question for the second time, "I have him. I will always have him."

"Where?"

He raised his eyes, now more red-rimmed than before and slowly filling with tears, "He's in an urn in my house."

"He is your partner."

"Yes, he is my part... was, my partner."

*****

Ernie was raised in Orange County, California. Another big Mexican bear of a man, he exudes confidence and laughs easily. He began his journey as a sworn officer in 1978. In 1985 he received his first dog, "Asco."

"I got Asco one week before we started training together to handle police work. He was to be one of our department's Police Service Dogs." Ernie said.

"The reason I got the dog before we started training was so we could bond. I took him home, he learned that I fed him, and we learned to trust each other. He learned that I was the alpha male and in charge. See, Robert, at that time most of the dogs were imported from West Germany. They are typically two or three years old when they come to the police agencies. They have already had a life. One week they are in Germany in 50-degree weather, next they are in a crate getting shipped on a plane to America. The next thing they know is they are in Riverside, California in 100-degree weather, at the Adlerhorst Kennel. This is German for Eagle's Nest. The language is different, the weather is different, and they are in culture shock. So, we get the dogs and they get accustomed to their new surroundings. Robert, this is a critical phase. When we go through training if the dog does not know his place in the pack he is just as likely to bite the handler as the suspect, thinking he is in charge."

"I see," I was now in a learning phase. Yes, I'd been a cop and had accompanied numerous dogs on searches for bad men, but little did I know of the background that went into the making of the "K-9" team.

"One of the training phases is to put a man in a bite suit (this is padding for the trainer to wear so he does not get hurt when the dog bites), and he then fires a blank from a gun. The dog is supposed to obey my command and subdue the man with my German order 'Fas.' During this phase of the training, when the trainer fired blanks from the gun, Asco ran the other way and hid. The trainer, 'Dave,' told me, 'Asco is done.'

"I couldn't believe it. My wife, Susanne, and I had in one week's time grown to love Asco. What didn't help was she and I were trying to have a baby. Asco had easily become part of our family. The thought of not having him around was devastating!

"I asked Dave, 'Can I work with him? Maybe we can fix him.'

"'No Ernie, Asco is done. He doesn't have the nerves, the temperament,' Dave said.

"'Let me work with him. Maybe he just needs a little time to get used to the gunfire. Maybe we can remediate him.'

"Dave looked at me, 'Ernie, you cannot give a dog nerves or temperament. You can teach him tactics and commands. It's not your fault. Asco will never be a Police Service Dog.'

"Asco knew me as Dad, his pack leader. How was I going to tell Susanne the newest member of our family was gone?

"Dave told me he had another dog for me. Robert, I didn't want another dog. First of all, I loved Asco. Secondly, we had already started training. I was a little worried about going into scenarios with a dog that didn't know me and recognize me as his alpha male… I took the dog. What else could I do? The department expected to have another K-9 on the department. I couldn't say 'No.' That would be like telling the department I was refusing an order. It's called insubordination."

*****

Ex Von Schimmel-Schulz Heide was born on June 26, 1982. He grew to be a large, strong, smart, one-hundred-pound German Shepherd.

*****

"Robert, when I first saw Ex all I thought of was Asco. But after a little while I got to know Ex, and we became partners. When your dog is on the leash he can feel his handler, pack leader, 'Dad,' on the other end. He knows he can trust you and you know you can trust him. I trusted Ex's hearing, and smell to tell me a suspect's location. It's a basic dog handler's rule. Trust your dog. It's like this, when you smell an apple pie, you smell an apple pie. Your dog smells apples, cinnamon, sugar, flour, and salt. Ex trusted me if he was engaged with a suspect and was getting hurt, that I was right there to assist him and save him from harm. Your dog grows to trust your judgment and that you would never send him into a situation he could not handle. Ex and I understood we were a team, a pack so to speak. We had explicit trust in each other and we would always help and protect each other. This trust was based on mutual respect and confidence."

*****

Ernie and "Ex" came out number one in their Basic Handler's Course at the Adlerhorst graduating on August 31, 1985.

*****

"It turns out although Ex was great at training and competitions, in the field, he kind of failed his first test."

Ernie looked at me and smiled reminiscing over the event. "One of the cops had just completed a field sobriety test on a drunk driver. I was backing him up. As the officer was moving to arrest him, the suspect spun and raised his fists to fight. I let Ex out of the back seat of our radio car as the officer took the suspect to the ground on his stomach. Ex just stood around wondering what to do. As the officer was handcuffing the suspect, Ex jumped on the suspect's back. He barked in a high pitch and just kind of scratched him."

"Ernie, what was Ex supposed to do?"

"I had given the order 'Fas!' Bite and hold. He had failed me, and I didn't know for sure what he would do under other dire circumstances. Ex needed some real-life experience."

"Ernie," I said, "This is just like a real-life partner."

Ernie smiled at me, "Yup."

"You never know if you can trust your partner until he proves it to you."

"Exactly."

"Ernie, I once had a trainee, and we had just arrested a guy for hitting someone in the head with a bottle. This was across the street from a nightclub where all his friends were. When we handcuffed the guy, about 20 of his friends sprinted across the street at us yelling and cursing us to let him go. My trainee was in front of me. I was putting out a call for assistance. As soon as I finished broadcasting, the first guy was on us. My trainee grabbed him by the head and drove him into the parking lot. The rest of the group froze and turned and ran the other way. Up to that point, I had no idea how my trainee would react under a very bad situation. I never doubted him or wondered how he would react after that."

Ernie looked at me with a huge grin, "Exactly. Robert, after going through the training and coming out number one, I felt Ex and I were confident, competent and capable of handling any critical incident involving any suspect. I used to tell the guys, 'If we can't handle it, I don't know who can.' But like I said, Ex needed a little field experience.

"Robert, by this time, Ex was part of our family. Susanne and I loved the dog. He was more than a police K-9 to us! As I said, we were trying to have a baby. In a manner of speaking, Ex was our kid, 'our baby.'"

Ernie laughed and said, "We had a kennel for the dog. He never spent one night there. He had the run of the backyard, or he was in the house with us. He was our spoiled kid. Although he was our kid, in the streets, we were partners. As a few months went by, Ex came to trust my judgment and obey my commands on patrol. By the beginning of the year 1986, he and I were a team in every sense of the word."

*****

"Susanne got pregnant right near the end of 1985. But there were problems." Ernie's eyes and face were now a mixture of emotion. "Let me tell you how much we loved Ex. In the middle of the night on March 17, 1986, Susanne started bleeding. Obviously, we had to get to the hospital. Our house was a hub of activity. Lights were on, we were getting dressed, I was calling my parents. Ex sensed the anxiety and was pacing around in the house as if he was wondering what he could do to help. As we were leaving the house, Susanne looked at me; we had the same thought… Ex. She said, 'Throw him in the Bronco.' Ex came with us to the hospital. That night Susanne lost the baby. As she and I were grieving, I remembered Ex had been locked up in the Bronco without a break. I asked Susanne if I could check on Ex in the Bronco. She wondered why I had left him locked up for so long.

"Susanne and I never got over the loss."

*****

"We got the call at 10:33 p.m. It was July 2, 1986. It was 80 degrees and balmy. As it so happened, both of the city's K-9 units were on duty and free to respond. It was a call of a man walking through the neighborhood firing a shotgun. Multiple residents had called, a sure indication it was for real."

I looked at Ernie, "It was a hot call."

"Oh yeah Robert, you know those calls. The ones that get you pretty keyed up right away. Minutes after the call came out,, an officer in the 800 block of Banyan Street saw the suspect with the shotgun. The suspect saw the officer and jumped over a fence into someone's backyard."

Ernie explained the layout of the call to me. The call came out the suspect was at the East 800 block of Banyan Street. This is in the City of Ontario. There are two cul de sacs coming off the 800 block of Banyan Street in a southern direction. Caldwell Street is on the west and Taylor Street is to the east. After a two-block perimeter had been set by several responding officers, Ernie parked his radio car on the corner of Banyan and Taylor. Ernie's fellow K-9 unit parked on the corner of

Banyan and Caldwell Place. So, they were on the same block, but on opposite corners facing each other. The house at Banyan Street and Taylor actually faces Taylor Street. So, the side of the house faces Banyan, where Ernie was parked. The side of the house has a two-foot block wall with a two-foot wrought iron fence topping it.

"I specifically chose two fellow officers, Steve and Brad, to accompany me on the search for the man shooting the shotgun. I chose both of those officers because they were very smart tactically. I told Steve to bring a shotgun. As an officer had seen the suspect jump over the block wall into the backyard of the house on the southwest corner of Banyan and Taylor, we were pretty sure the suspect was within our two-block perimeter. Since the sides of the two northernmost houses face Banyan, and all our radio cars were on Banyan, and we had all our lights focused on the side of both houses, and we could not see anything, I opted to not search the north side of this house. I mean the suspect would not be right under our noses, right?"

I looked at Ernie.

"I know, Robert. That was my first mistake."

Steve, Brad, Ex and I started searching the backyard of the house I was parked in front of. When we got to the backyard, Ex alerted by running back and forth along the block wall. His nose was in the air, and he was wagging his tail as he ran. But there was nothing there. It was a wall. There were no bushes there, no tree to hide in, nothing. I called Ex to continue searching, but he kept going back to the block wall at the rear of the house. I wasn't frustrated with Ex, I just couldn't figure out why he kept going to the block wall. Robert, the other side of the block wall is the side of the house I had not searched. The side of the house that was open facing Banyan Street."

Ernie had just told me to trust your dog; rule number one, remember? I told him so.

"I know, Robert. It was my second mistake. But surely I thought the suspect wouldn't be hiding in the side yard bushes next to several police officers. He would have kept running like most suspects."

He sighed. I could tell he was reliving the event. I had been on too many searches to not live it with him.

"I got Ex away from the block wall and we continued our search south for three more houses. While at the fourth house, a civilian crime scene evidence collector noticed a shirt on the fence bordering Banyan Street. He walked over to get the shirt and a man in the bushes bordering the wall opposite where Ex alerted raised a shotgun at him."

"Ernie, this is the side of the house you didn't search."

Ernie had that look. I've had the look before. All cops have. It's the look that tells everyone we know we screwed up. Most of the time, we get away with it. Nothing bad happens. Sometimes though, our screw-ups are very, very costly.

"Yeah, Robert."

"Look, Ernie, I know you and all the cops had the side of the house lit up. You couldn't see him?"

"No, Robert, he was deep in some bushes. No one saw him. There were a lot of guys around, but no one knew exactly where he had hidden. No one saw him. But when he raised the shotgun from out of the bushes, the sergeant saw where he was. He saw the movement in the bushes and the shotgun being raised at an unarmed evidence technician. In that brief moment the sergeant couldn't fire, he didn't have a clear shot, the evidence technician was in the way."

I looked at Ernie; we understood. It was for real time. I'd been in circumstances. Circumstances where I did not shoot, but could have. Where the guy had a gun. Circumstances where he had just minutes before fired his gun. Then I found him and was face to face with him. And he had a gun. I understood.

"I put Ex on the leash. Steve, Brad, Ex and I ran back to the north side yard of the first house we searched. The house I was parked next to. The side of the house I didn't search. All of us sidled on the side of the house, west toward the bushes where the asshole was hiding. We still could not see him. It had been just over an hour and a half now since we had arrived. I was hot and sweaty. I had been searching with Ex using all my mental concentration. Ex had been right on when he alerted earlier on the empty wall. The suspect had been on the other side, and he had smelled him through the block wall. I hadn't trusted my dog."

Ladies and gentlemen, just to let you know, being keyed up for that long, expecting at any instant a man with a shotgun might fire at you, is very, very, very, exhausting.

"I had some choices. Options. We now knew where he was. I could wait and call S.W.A.T. I was thinking though this would take too much time, and we were in a fluid situation. The thing was he had just pointed the shotgun at one of our guys. No telling what he would do. I wanted us to win. I wanted Ex and I to get the bad guy, to be heroes. I decided to use a diversion. I decided to blind the suspect with all our lights so he couldn't see us coming. Then I would send in Ex to incapacitate him, and we would arrest him.

"Robert, I gave Steve and Brad explicit instructions. Stay right behind me. After Ex grabs the suspect, we'll rush to apprehend him.

"They were great cops and instinctively knew what to do. I crept around a bush exposing ourselves in the open area of the side yard. Again, Ex alerted. His ears were up, he had located the suspect's fear scent. He was completely focused on the bushes in front of us. We were about twenty feet away from the bushes where the helicopter last saw the suspect hiding. I gave my partner the command, "Fas" and Ex took off into the bushes. Ex had him, he was pulling him out. My partner, my best friend, and family member, beloved by my wife and I, he who trusted me had the suspect. In an instant, I was running to help him. Then it happened. I simultaneously saw and heard the muzzle flash. Then the shotgun blast. As I went to the ground, I could hear and feel the gravel of the rocks beneath me. I wondered if I was shot. I thought, 'This is it, I am going to die. God help me, my wife, my mother, my grandmother in heaven help me.' It was like a movie where I was watching my life frame by frame, all these hundreds of thoughts flooding my head. And I could see them all separately and so clear. Panic had set in, 'Fuck I can't see the suspect, I don't know where he is, I'm dead.' I started diving into the gravel. As I was seeing all this and thinking all this, I suddenly got really really angry. And before I hit the gravel I thought, 'Fuck you! I'm going to get you!' So, from the time it took me to start diving to the gravel, till before I hit the gravel, I had gone from complete panic to unbelievable rage. Before I hit the gravel, I was shooting. All six of my bullets. It was all I had. 'I'm going to live, you're going to die!' I was shooting into the bushes where I thought the suspect was. I was aware there was gunfire to my left also. A second later I looked at my partner that I loved like a son, Ex, who trusted me. Who trusted me to save him if he was getting hurt. He was motionless. Blood. He was motionless in a pool of blood. I screamed, 'YOU MOTHERFUCKER, YOU KILLED MY DOG!!!' It was too much, too much for me to handle. Grief and rage mixed together and overcame me. My mind was working, 'How can I fix this, I can set the clock back, I can do this again, let me set the clock back, we'll do it right next time.' I was crying, sobbing uncontrollably and I was crawling. I was completely out of my head; full of anguish and rage, all mixed up together. I got to this fucking asshole and started trying to hit him. I was crying and hysterical and out of my mind as I was hitting him. But it did no good. I felt no better. I felt crushed inside as Ex lay motionless next to me. I think I only hit him a couple of times, but I was hoping each of my blows would kill him.

"Robert, I sent him to his death. Ex trusted me, and I killed him."

What could I tell Ernie?

"I later learned the sergeant heard Ex cry one time and then he was gone. After I got to the suspect, the sergeant had two fellow cops pick me up and carry me away. I fired six rounds. Steve fired two rounds from the shotgun, and Brad fired five. Both Brad and Steve believed that when I went to the ground, I had been shot. I later asked Brad why he only fired five rounds when he had six in his gun."

"'Ernie,' he said, 'I didn't know if we got the suspect. If we hadn't, I wanted one round in my gun to finish him.'

"I told you Robert, he was a smart guy.

"I fired six rounds. Brad fired five. Steve fired two, and the suspect fired one round. That's fourteen rounds. It lasted about five seconds. I was 29 years old.

"The suspect was shot once in the arm and once in the leg. He was in a prone position, and we were firing over him. He later sued us for excessive use of force. He was on angel dust, P.C.P. and had a blood alcohol content of 2.1. Imagine that. He was walking around a residential neighborhood shooting a shotgun. He's high on P.C.P., he points a shotgun at us and then claims we overreacted.

"I've second guessed myself over and over. I now believe I should have waited. We had him contained. I should have called in S.W.A.T. We could not see him. He could see us. He had all the advantages.

"The department was divided. Officers, humans had been killed in the line of duty. They received the Medal of Valor. Half the officers in the department thought Ex should have received the Medal of Valor, half did not. Some felt he was just a dog. Ex was much more than that. He gave his life in exchange for mine and the officers with me. He saved our lives with his last heroic act. My dog should have received the Medal of Valor posthumously. He saved my life and took the blast for me. He never received recognition for what he did. He really was a hero.

"I didn't want to go back to being a K-9 handler. Dave from Adler Horst insisted.

"'Ernie,' he said, 'you can't go out like this. I got another dog for you. Look, this wasn't your fault, and you can't end it like this.'

"Robert, we were going to Germany. Ex and I for K-9 competition along with Dave. Then in typical cop sarcasm, Dave said, 'We lost the best team member,' he looked at me and said, 'Not you!'

"I took another dog.

"The suspect was charged with attempted murder on a police officer, and killing a police dog. He pled guilty to assault with a deadly weapon on a police officer and spent less than a year in county jail.

"My wife and I were grieving after losing our baby. Again, we grieved together after losing another family member. We were alone together. I was mad at her for not helping me through my grieving, too immature to understand she could not help me. She was lost in her own grief over both the baby and Ex and could barely help herself much less me. Six months later we separated and divorced."

I finished getting Ernie's story and begged him for a drink. He fixed us both a Vodka Cranberry. As I was driving home on the freeway unable to stop the tears rolling down my cheeks, I got a phone call. It was Ernie.

I violated the law and answered the call. He was jovial. "Hey Robert, I forgot to tell you something."

"What?"

"There was this lieutenant who always had some dog biscuits for Ex and the other police dog, Carlos. He always gave Ex a biscuit every day before we went on duty. After I got my new dog, he continued the practice. One day a new sergeant went into the lieutenant's office and saw the container of dog biscuits. He took one, thinking it was a cookie. The lieutenant let the sergeant eat the biscuit. After eating the biscuit, he told the lieutenant it was pretty tasty. Well, word spread about the incident and the guys made up a sign. They placed it around my new dog's neck. It read, 'Sergeant, Please, stop eating my cookies.' They took a picture of the dog with the sign around his neck, and the story spread to everyone at the station."

I drove home laughing so hard I thought I would pee myself while at the same time crying.

Chapter 8

Norco

Fourth St. and Hamner Ave., Norco, CA

When I was in the academy, we studied this shooting. Shooting... HAH, this was more than a shooting; it was an epic event. There are so many different facets to this story it is impossible to tell it all in one chapter. So I will not. To tell the tale from one person's account is like taking three blind men to an elephant and asking them to describe it after touching a part of it. Of course, one person who touches the tusks will say an elephant is long, hard, and pointy. Another who touches the trunk will say he is like a long hairy snake with two big holes at the end of it. And a third, who touches the leg, will tell you he is like a tree trunk, thick, round, and bristly.

I will tell you this story from one person's account. That's what this book is about. You can only imagine what the others in the event were feeling or went through. It is as harrowing a tale now as when I first heard it.

It was a bullet party and everybody was invited.

*****

When I first met Rolf I was reminded of young William Shatner. Not in his mannerisms, but in his looks. Not a bad thing, huh? Rolf laughs all the time, except when we sat down and he told me what happened on the afternoon of May 9, 1980.

*****

Rolf is a Long Beach, California boy. He grew up in a middle-class home in Belmont Shores. Now those homes are going for over a million dollars. From Belmont Shores, it was a walk of several blocks to the beach. As a teen, Rolf was either in shorts, flip-flops and a tee shirt, or in shorts, flip-flops and no tee shirt. He was happy living by the southern California beach, surfing and body surfing. He has been going to the beach and playing handball now for 45 years. He loves the sun, fresh ocean air, and the bikinis. As he describes it, "It was a fun city."

Rolf's mother had been divorced for many years. When he was seventeen, she remarried a military man, a man who was about duty to country. This influenced Rolf immensely and made him want to contribute. His mother and stepfather made many sacrifices for him. He said his parents are members of Tom Brokaw's, "Greatest Generation." (This is referring to the generation who went through the great depression and through World War II).

Rolf was attending college in 1971. At this time the Vietnam War was hot and heavy. Many of Rolf's friends had already gone to Vietnam. He was sure to go, and he decided he would go on his own terms as an officer, specifically a pilot. Four years later the war was winding down, and they were downsizing the military. Rolf found himself studying to be a pilot without a war to go to. He got his commercial pilot's license. Nevertheless, Rolf found himself as a young man of 20 years, working as an Emergency Medical Technician as an ambulance operator in Long Beach while finishing up his degree. He had already been married a year. Rolf was assigned to the downtown area of Long Beach. In this area, they got so busy often there were no available fire/paramedics to assist them and Rolf learned how to make decisions without supervision. Shooting victims, stabbing victims, and car accidents were constant calls. By his 21st birthday, Rolf had seen enough blood and guts to last a lifetime.

Rolf joined the Signal Hill Police Department as a reserve police officer in 1976. He was 23 years old. He attended the reserve Los Angeles County Sheriff's Academy. On August 31, 1977, he accepted a position as a Riverside County Deputy Sheriff where he went through a second academy, the Riverside County Sheriff's Academy. He was now 24 years old and while working and supporting his wife, still had the time and energy to earn his bachelor's degree. In today's society, one would say up to this point in his life he was a determined, responsible, focused young man with solid life experience. Someone dependable, reliable and trustworthy.

*****

Riverside County is the fourth largest county in the state of California with 7,208 square miles. One of the patrol areas was the Corona/Norco team where Rolf was assigned. Norco stood for North Corona.

In 1980 he was living in Long Beach. All of Rolf's family and friends lived there. He wanted to be closer to home, so he applied to different police agencies, mainly in Orange County. The Irvine Police Department gave him a job offer on May 7, 1980. That same day he gave his resignation to the Riverside County Sheriff's Department, asking for his last day to be May 17, 1980. He was to start with the Irvine Police Department on May 19, 1980.

"Robert, my boss accepted my resignation. He was happy for me. He started telling me about the Irvine Police Department and what great opportunities there would be for me.

"On Friday, May 9, 1980, two days after turning in my resignation, I was working what was called the cover watch, from noon to ten p.m. We had briefing before we hit the streets. I was normally assigned to Norco. Deputy Bolasky normally worked the county area. On that day we heard rumors there would be a riot at the Rubidoux High School, which was in the county's patrol area. During briefing, right after we found out about the potential riot, Deputy Bolasky who was sitting in front of me, turned in his seat and said to me, 'I'm working Norco today, you're working Rubidoux.'"

Rolf was laughing as he told me this. I could see where this was going, I was laughing too. As Rolf recounted this, he said to me, "He had seniority over me. He could choose where he wanted to work. I thought to myself, 'Alright, alright, that's the seniority system.' What choice did I have?" By now Rolf and I were cracking up laughing. "That's just how fate worked for both Bolasky and me.

"I remember that when the call went out, I was on a car stop. I was citing the driver right on a street next to Rubidoux High School. I wanted everyone to see that the Sheriff's Department was in the area so if there was going to be a riot, they would think twice about it. I'd just started writing the ticket. I was seven or eight miles north and east of Norco. In those days when a hot call went out, we had a special tone, like a 'Beeeeep,' that would precede the call to let us know to pay attention. Our dispatcher that day, Gary, had been a deputy sheriff who was forced into retirement on a medical pension. He was very experienced and very cool and calm throughout the incident. The call came out as a robbery in progress at the Security Pacific Bank at Fourth and Hamner in Norco. This was the southeast corner of Fourth and Hamner. The bank is no longer there. It caught my attention. It was different than a robbery silent alarm."

Folks, it's important that you understand this. Robbery silent alarm calls go out all the time. They get your attention because of the potential for danger. Most of the time though, someone has bumped the alarm button by mistake. A large number of them are false alarms. But when the call comes out as a 'robbery in progress,' you have a different animal on your hands. Most of those are real. You can probably bet if the call comes out that it is a 'robbery in progress' at a bank, there are guns involved. That call will get your attention.

"I'm going, 'Oh shit, he's there by himself,' meaning Bolasky. There are probably no other cars in the area. As soon as the initial call goes out, Bolasky broadcasts he is at the location. 'WOW,' I thought, he's right on top of this thing. Right after Bolasky's broadcast, I hear other radio transmissions that other Norco cars responding. Deputy Hille, another unit, is rolling and other cars too. Right after I hear that transmission, within seconds, I hear Bolasky shouting and screaming he's been shot at, and he's under fire. By the inflection in his voice, you could hear he is completely panicked. You could tell he was in a bad position. Gary, dispatch, repeats it cool as can be. Bolasky gets on the radio again, 'I'm getting shot at, we need to get people out here, I need help.' He was completely panicked. I ran to the guy who I was citing and gave him back his license. 'I gotta go. Here's your stuff.' The guy was staring at me like, 'What just happened?' I sprinted to my car and took off west on Limonite.

"I was going balls to the wall, Bolasky was screaming. Then there would be little pauses on the radio. The next thing he was transmitting was he'd been hit. He was screaming bloody murder. He was panicked to the max. You could feel and hear a sense of doom from his voice. He had been shooting at them, and they had been shooting at him. Other units are rolling, other cars are transmitting over units, and I'm rolling, rolling hot. The car is hitting dips so hard I'm going airborne when I come off them. It was like that scene out of the movie Bullitt, that car chase. The car is bottoming out, boom, boom, boom. I mean, at this point you do not care about the car, it is secondary. Secondary to getting there alive. I was braking so hard my brakes were getting hot, so hot it was getting hard to stop at intersections. As soon as the intersections were clear I would then accelerate pedal to the metal. Bolasky is still on the air; he is saying he needs help. He needs the Marines, the Air Force, anybody. Hille comes on the air and transmits he has arrived at Bolasky's location, which was east of the bank. He immediately starts getting shot at. Bolasky is on the air and sounds like if he doesn't get to the hospital, he is going to die. People are screaming on the air. It was pandemonium."

"Rolf, what are you looking for when you get there? Who is giving you information about the suspects? Or the vehicles?"

"We were getting information from people calling the station, civilians. Gary, our dispatcher, was putting it out. What we knew was five different men were shooting at the deputies. We knew they were in a blue van. What we didn't know was when Bolasky shot at the van, one of his shotgun pellets hit the driver. The van was driving away at the time the driver was shot. It paralyzed the driver and eventually killed him. When Bolasky shot the driver, the van crashed into a fence. So, I knew the van had crashed.

"By now Deputy Delgado had arrived on Hamner Ave., across the street north of the bank, north of Fourth Street. Delgado was shooting at the suspects from about 60 yards away. When the van crashed, the suspects got out of the side doors, on the right side and ran to Hamner. While this is happening, Hille radioed he had retrieved Bolasky and was taking him to the hospital. Delgado is now alone at the scene. He radios that four suspects hijacked a yellow utility truck on Hamner and have taken two people hostage. He also radios their last seen direction was north on Hamner Ave."

"Rolf, this is as amazing now as when I first heard the story. How much time has gone by now?"

"Four minutes, four minutes from the time the call went out till the time they stole the utility truck. A fourth deputy, Deputy Reed was driving south on Hamner to get to the scene. As he passed the suspects, they shot a fusillade of bullets at him from the bed of the truck and back seat of the truck. He transmitted he was hit. Robert, this was unreal. Everybody had been shot at or shot. No one had stopped these guys. It was unreal. How was it we could not stop them? It was really scary. I was rolling down the road, I was scared, and I was thinking, 'I'm on my last couple of days here. I don't need this.' I'm not even in the battle yet and I'm hearing something is worse than I can even imagine. Hille is talking on the radio that he's taking Bolasky to the hospital and Bolasky is bleeding profusely; he's even giving out Bolasky's blood type. I was under the impression he was near death. It was terrifying."

I could see the emotion in Rolf's eyes as he talked, the events so real to him now even thirty-three years later.

"Delgado was coordinating units to the bank at his location because he thought there were still suspects in the area. Things were confusing to say the least. By this time, I'm still about five miles away from the bank. I hear on the radio a roadblock is being set up at Hamner and Limonite. I was still westbound on Limonite nearing Etiwanda, still east of the incident. I decided to go south on Etiwanda then west on Holmes as an alternate route. I pulled to the right and parked facing south on Holmes just north of Wineville. I knew they were coming my way. Things were happening very fast. I was thinking, 'No one has stopped these guys yet. Why? If they are taking out all these radio cars, what am I going to do?' I was alone, and I felt alone. Everyone they had encountered was out of action. It was a hopeless feeling. I knew this was going to happen to me too unless I did something. The only thing is that I didn't know what to do. I had no answers. I was locked up, my thinking. I'm in my car, and then I saw them coming."

"What were you thinking?"

"Well, I saw an 'orange' utility truck. Remember it had been broadcast that it was a yellow utility truck. So, I was thinking, maybe it was not the suspects. I didn't want to encounter them alone. I had to come to grips with the situation. As they rounded the corner, I see them, and I hear gunfire. I didn't know it yet, but they were shooting at Deputy Borden who is out of my sight around a curve in the road. It was a barrage. There were so many rounds being unloaded and shot so fast I couldn't believe it. OH… MY… GOD… I realized it's them. They are shooting out of the back of the utility truck and are coming my way, but they just haven't seen me yet. Borden broadcasted he had been fired upon and has crashed his car. I was now petrified. I was running scenarios through my head. I thought as they approached me, I might gun my car and race past them. I was thinking they might crash their car into my car and disable me then kill me. I was trying to think of things I could do to not to get shot. I had parked my car too close to a fence, and I couldn't get out of the right side if I wanted to. I started wondering if I was going to live. I rolled up my window."

Rolf now laughed, "It seems ridiculous, but I wanted to get as much of a barrier between them and myself as I could. I wanted a hole to crawl into, but there was none. I had just seen them unload on Borden. I knew what was coming. Their rate of fire was devastating. I decided I would make myself as small a target as possible. Instinctively I leaned to my right over the bench seat and put my left arm over the side of my head. I thought if I could just protect my head, I would maybe survive. Maybe I would only get shot in my arm. In this position, I could see with my right eye just a little bit. As the truck approached, you could hear the rounds hitting my car. Bam, bdabum all over the car. Some of the guns sounded like a cannon going off. Some of the guns had a loud crack. From the intensity of the fire, I thought it was machine gun fire. But they were all single action; they did not have machine guns. At this point, there was no thought of fighting. I was just trying not to die. Things went into slow motion. Forever and ever you could hear the shots, the sound of the rounds and then the sound of the bullets hitting the car. I focused on the image of my wife. Then I wondered, and the thought is as clear to me now as it was then, 'Is it going to hurt to die?' Amid so many bullets striking the car I knew it was going to happen. No one could survive the amount of bullets coming through the car. They were now driving by. And as they were, it seemed like they were driving so slow, I could see their faces in the truck. As I was leaned over with my left arm covering all my head, I could barely see them out of the window with my right eye. Distinctly I could see their faces, in slow motion. They were looking down at me as they drove by and they were aiming their rifles at me and shooting at me trying to kill me. They were hairy. They had long hair, beards, mustaches, twenty-five-year-old white guys. Then the car was flying apart, my car, pieces of the car were flying, flying around. It was almost like snow slowly falling down around me. Like a slow-moving blizzard. Then all of sudden it happened, BAM, it hit my head, (at this point Rolf slammed his hand down on the table, simulating the force of the impact to his head). The force of the impact moved my head. I thought, 'Fuck! Okay, that's one. I'm still alive, when's the next one coming?' Weird though, I never felt pain until a couple of hours later. I think it was the adrenaline blocking the pain. I was waiting for the next one to hit me, and I wondered again, 'Is it going to hurt to die?' I knew it was going to happen. I just wondered if it was going to hurt. I was holding my breath. From the time they started shooting at my car till they passed me was probably two to three seconds."

"Rolf, two to three seconds to have all those thoughts and get shot and know you were going to die. Amazing!"

"Robert, as they were shooting at me I could see them. They had to be able to see me. I saw their eyes looking at me, aiming with the rifles. I was taking glass in my face, in my hair, in my right eye. After they passed me, they kept shooting at me. You could hear the shots getting fainter and fainter, but the bullets are still hitting my car. They are hitting the pavement around me. When they made a little turn in the road, they could no longer see me, and they stopped shooting. I sat up. I checked myself. I brushed some of the glass out of my hair. I could feel a furrow on the top of my head where I'd been shot. My rear window was shot out, but strangely enough, the driver's window was intact. They had been shooting in the door itself, in the metal. The only thing I heard then was the sound of the engine running. It's weird the sound of the engine was comforting to me. Like, 'We made it! My car and I made it.' And then I thought, 'I'm leaving in a few days. I don't need this! Do I need any of this shit? No one would blame me if I just got out of my car and walked home.' Time was now back to normal." At this point, Rolf and I were busting up laughing.

"But Robert, it was a serious thought. It was only for several seconds, but I seriously thought, I should just go home."

"Did you get mad when they were shooting at you?"

"No. I was frightened they were going to kill me. They had me, I was just waiting to die, and after the shooting stopped I actually said to myself, 'You're not dead! You're supposed to be dead!' I couldn't believe it. I was checking myself out; I was checking my legs, they worked. I was still in fighting condition. I finally realized I was okay. A couple of more seconds had gone by. Again, I had the thought, 'Am I going to stay in this fight, or am I not going to stay in this fight?' When I looked down the road, there was no one there, no one to fight the bad guys. I thought of Bolasky, possibly dead. I thought, 'What would he do if these guys killed me? Would he go after the guys who killed me?' That's when I decided, 'I'm in this for the ride. No way could I let these guys get away.' I thought these things while at the same time realizing I might not live through the day."

"So, you made the decision to get back in the fight, realizing you might die?"

"Yeah, everybody is out of commission, no one was left, at least that I knew of. This is a continued thought that developed more and more as the event wore on. And you see this in war movies all the time. Soldiers talk about it, how they know they are going to die. It was just a matter of when. That's how it was for me. I slowly made a U-turn, I was alone, the radio was silent. No one was coming to help me. I thought then I was the only one who could engage the suspects. I went back up Holmes to follow them. As I got close to Etiwanda, I saw them. As soon as I saw them, they started shooting at me. I could hear the rounds hitting the ground around me. I could not hear the gunshots, but I could hear this snapping sound all around my car and behind my car. Like someone snapping a bullwhip, that's the best way I can describe the sound. I thought someone was behind me shooting at me. I turned around, and there was no one there. And although I had seen the rifles shooting at me, it hadn't sunk in till this moment. 'They have rifles!' No one had said anything up until now that the suspects had rifles. This is unusual even for a bank robbery from this time era as 100% of the time all bank robberies we knew of were committed with revolvers and shotguns."

Rolf pointed in the distance, "See that row of bushes?"

"Yeah."

"That's how far away they were from me."

"Rolf, that's two football fields away!"

"Yeah! I couldn't believe it. They were shooting at me and fairly accurate too from that distance. Lots of rounds were hitting behind me. I got on the air, 'They've got rifles.'"

"Rolf, you had seen the rifles."

"Yeah, I had seen them, but I had so many things going through my head like, 'Am I going to stay in the shootout?' That it hadn't dawned on me till then. They were now going north on Etiwanda. My heart was still pounding. Breathing was interesting. I had to tell myself to breathe. I hadn't realized I'd been holding my breath. I was now transmitting the pursuit. Ten minutes had passed from the time of the bank robbery until now.

"I later gave a presentation on the robbery. I got pretty choked up at this point in the story. I cried in front of fifty people… I guess thinking you are going to die is a very solemn thing. My car was my coffin. I had accepted giving up my life, and all they had to do was take it. Since I didn't die, my life started again at that point."

"Did you tell them you had been shot?"

"No."

"Did you make a conscious decision to not tell anyone you had been shot?"

"Yeah."

"Why?"

"I didn't want them taking me out of the fight."

"So you decided not to tell anyone you were shot so you could stay in the action?"

"Yes."

"But it took you a little bit to get to that point."

In a soft voice, Rolf answered, "Yeah.

"Anyway, like I said, they were again shooting at me, and I could hear the rounds snapping around my car. I'm thinking, 'Oh shit they can still kill me.' I laid down again on the bench seat with my left hand on the steering wheel. I propped myself up just far enough so I could just barely see out of the windshield and chased them. That's how I drove. Deputy Brown, who was an academy classmate of mine, turned south on Etiwanda from Limonite. The rounds were hitting my car now. I could hear and feel them hitting the radiator and the body of the car. When they saw Brown, all three suspects turned in unison and started firing at his car. I could just see Brown's radio car exploding. Glass was flying everywhere. They crossed Limonite Ave. Brown was hit and out of the chase. I drove up to Deputy Brown, and I'm talking to him on the radio, 'Are you alright, are you alright?' He sits up and starts brushing glass off himself and checking himself with his hands. He says, 'I'm okay, I'm hit in the leg.' I thought, 'Should I get out of the car and check on him or continue the chase?' I was aware there was shooting but not too aware the suspects were firing at Deputies McDaniels and Madden who were also at the intersection at Limonite and Etiwanda in separate cars. To give you some perspective I was checking on Brown while the suspects were shooting at McDaniels and Madden and it all took place in about three to four seconds. McDaniels was hit. He was out of the chase. I again took off. All the deputies' cars were now shot up and were just sitting there. I now realize I can't engage. I just want to keep them in sight. I can't fight back. I kept a far distance from them now, but they were still shooting. I was leaned over again with just my eyes peeking over the windshield. I then saw the windshield open. A hole appeared with glass flakes falling in. I actually could see one of the suspects in an aiming position in the back of the truck aiming his rifle right at me. It was a bullet coming through the windshield. It whizzed right over my head. I thought, 'OH MY GOD, they got me dialed in. They're going to kill me. They can aim, and kill me!!!' Again I thought, 'I **AM** dead.' I thought, 'I've got to think tactically. As long as I can see them, that is what's important.' I stopped the radio car and waited. I let them get some distance in front of me."

"That's smart, Rolf," I said.

Rolf gave me a smile, and in a lilting voice said while laughing, "Buuut, we've got these Highway Patrol guys who drive up to me and pass me, balls to the wall. I figured these guys are goners. They have no idea what they're getting into. They are driving into the buzz saw. I was leaned over so far trying to become invisible. The suspects turned right on Jurupa Road followed by the Chippies (California Highway Patrol or CHP). I turned right, or east onto 58th Street. I needed a breather. I had just seen the windshield open up with this huge hole, and had a bullet whiz by my head. I had no direct radio contact with the Chippies and could not warn them. I decided to go north on Marlatt to try and stay close to them. I turned north on Marlatt and there they were. The orange truck followed by the Chippies in two cars. We were all taking fire. I was hanging back as far as I could, but I was still taking fire. Deputy Madden was behind me. He radioed to me, 'Rolf your front tire is shot out.' I'm still ducked down as far as I could and still see to drive. He said, 'Pull over and I'll pick you up.' I partially sat up and could see my gas gauge was empty. I thought they shot out my gas tank. I stopped, but Madden doesn't stop. He keeps going."

Rolf laughed. I couldn't tell if it was from frustration in reliving the incident or if it was funny to him.

"Rolf, how were you feeling at this point? I mean they'd been shooting at you constantly now for what must have seemed like hours. Were you scared?"

"My feelings had evolved, changed. I must say I was determined. I had gone away from fear. By now they had done just too much fucking damage. They had shot my academy classmate, Brown. Guys were going to the hospital. I thought maybe Bolasky was dead. 'Too much fucking damage.' No way, there was no way I was going to let these guys get away. The fire was so intense that guys were broadcasting they had automatic weapons. Deputy Chisolm, who was new to patrol, was behind us and trying to catch up to the pursuit. He pulled up to me and picked me up. I didn't really know him. I got my shotgun and got into his car. His gear was everywhere scattered inside the car. Obviously, he had been driving like a bat out of hell."

Folks, understand I had heard this story several times before. One time in the academy, and another when I was lucky enough to gain access to a D.V.D. describing the incident. But as Rolf told me the story from his point of view, I was incredulous. It seemed to me there were patrol cars everywhere engaging these guys, but no one could stop them.

"Before I got picked up by Chisolm the suspects had made their way north on Dodd Street. When they got to Bellgrave Ave., Deputies Romo, Reynard, and CHP Officer Crowe were driving east on Bellgrave approaching Dodd Street. The suspects turned east on Bellgrave in front of the units and started firing on them. All three units were disabled. Crowe and Reynard were shot. CHP Officer Ernest, who had been following the suspects, stopped to help the wounded. By now Chisolm and I are north on Marlatt coming up to Bellgrave. We hear panic on the radio from different deputies; they're screaming they have been shot. When we turn right on Bellgrave, we see all these black, and white radio cars all shot up at Dodd Street. They were strewn in different places on the street, obviously disabled. We passed the cars because Deputy Madden was now at Bellgrave and Bain at a grocery store east of the shot-up deputies and chippie. He radioed that he believed the suspects were in the liquor store."

"Rolf, give me a time frame here. How fast were things happening?"

"Robert, things were happening in seconds. It was this street, then that street, east then north then west. It was crazy. If you were close to, well let's not even say close to the suspects, IF YOU WERE EVEN IN THEIR VIEW, YOU WERE GETTING SHOT AT! Bullets were hitting your car and the street around you. So, I get to one street west of Bain at Bellgrave, and I low crawled, cradling my shotgun in my hands through waist-high brush in the dirt to get to the rear of the liquor store where they said they were. While I'm crawling from a block away, Madden cleared the store. He yelled out it was clear. I then realized there was no one following the suspects. No one was broadcasting. All the units that had encountered the suspects were out of commission."

I looked at Rolf. It was just incredible to me three suspects had disabled so many deputies and their cars. I say three because one of the suspects, the fourth, was driving and not shooting.

"There was a City of Riverside helicopter in the air following them. The suspects were driving through the streets going in different directions. No units were following them. They eventually made their way to Etiwanda and drove north toward the 60 Freeway. The helicopter was broadcasting the location of the suspects, but they were getting the streets wrong. In trying to follow the helicopter's directions, we made about four or five complete donuts at the intersection of Van Buren and Bellgrave, code three (indicating driving with their red lights and siren on), with all these cars going by. We were trying to adjust to the helicopter's directions. Finally, I told Chisolm to stop. We stopped in the middle of the intersection. I ignored the helicopter's broadcasts and just looked up to see where he was. I figured if I could see where the helicopter was, I could locate the suspects. Finally, the helicopter broadcasted the suspects were on Old Mission and getting on the 60 Freeway. Old Mission is Van Buren Boulevard. That's the street we were doing donuts on. Now I knew where the suspects were. We drove north on Van Buren and got on the freeway. We went west on the 60 Freeway."

"Where was Madden?"

"He was helping the three deputies who were shot at Bellgrave and Dodd. It was total chaos. It was a complete fog of war. You had to follow the trail of crumbs. No one knew what was going on. Everybody is shot, or their cars are shot up. The suspects had shot at civilians, people are pointing, the helicopter is telling us they're going east, then west; it was a mess."

"And Chisolm, did he ever notice you were shot or did he ever tell you, 'You're shot, or are you okay?'"

"Honestly, Robert, he was scared out of his mind. He knew it was for real. He heard the panicked deputies on the radio and saw the units shot up. He was new to patrol, he had nothing to draw on, no experience. Actually, this was new to everyone. I think everyone was scared. He kept asking me as we drove around, 'Is that them? Is that them? There they are!'"

"I kept yelling at him, **'That's not them!'** As we drove west on the 60, I saw them. I yelled out **'THAT'S THEM!'** as I pointed to the orange truck. They weren't shooting at us at first. As we followed them to the north 15 Freeway, I told Chisolm to slow down, to give these guys some room. 'Let's keep them in sight but not too close so they can kill us.' Then they started shooting at us. I told Chisolm, 'Turn off the light bar, the emergency lights, so they don't have a target!' Their fire was accurate. They were hitting us from a moving truck on the freeway! Chisolm was overcome with fear. He keeps saying, 'Find me my helmet. No matter what you have to do, **FIND ME MY HELMET!'** He doesn't even remember this. I'm telling him, 'It's not going to do you any good. It's plastic.' So here I was digging through his gear that was scattered all on the floor. Bullets are coming through our windshield, hitting the car, hitting the freeway, you could actually hear them hitting the freeway, and I gave him his helmet. As I handed it to him, I told him, **'Here… it's not going to do you any good!'** They were firing at us from about a half-mile away. It was incredible. The fire was relentless. It never stopped. It was like if one guy ran out of ammo another would fire until he was out, then the third would start again while the other two reloaded. They never stopped firing.

"Now, picture this: Chisolm and I are hunkered down in the center of the bench seat together. I am leaning on my left elbow below the windshield, and he is leaning on his right elbow right in front of me. So, the front of my head is behind his neck and back. He is just barely peeking over the dash to see where he was driving. I was well beyond the fear stage, I was still angry. There were probably thirty police cars behind us now. They were from many different agencies. The shooting stopped. I guess the Chippies thought they were out of ammo because just then a California Highway Patrol unit came along the right side of us. I rolled my window down and yelled to him on the freeway, 'They have rifles.' He nodded at me. Then drove ahead of us."

"How'd you feel about that?"

"I was angry. This was my chase. Not his. Our guys, my friends had been shot up. I was in charge. Not the Chippies. I didn't want to get killed, but I didn't want to give them the lead, control. I told Chisolm to catch up to him, but not to pass him. I thought if he was going to get himself killed, okay, but we would stay a back a little ways. This is when, suddenly out of nowhere, I saw an explosion in the sky. It was about twenty yards in front of us and between our unit and the Chippies' unit. So, this bomb blasts and you feel the shrapnel hit the car. We were peppered with it. It was like if someone took a handful of rocks and threw them at our car. I thought I was facing gunfire, now I realized I was facing explosions. I radioed an explosive device had been thrown at us. Things were not getting better. Just when I thought things were getting better with all the help showing up, things only got worse. Now they were throwing grenades. Just then here came another explosion, number two. Things just kept getting worse. If I was scared before, now I was terrified. They were throwing bombs, and I didn't know what to do. At about this time steam started coming out of our hood. I told Chisolm to stay in the chase as long as possible. Then they started shooting at us again. The car started bucking, like a bucking bronco. The suspects got off the Sierra Highway off-ramp, and they threw another bomb. Chisolm had his foot all the way to the floor, but the car just slowed down and came to a stop at the Sierra Highway off-ramp. All the police cars were passing us to keep up with the pursuit. I was pissed. It was my chase. A CHP officer stopped to pick us up. I declined."

"Why?"

Rolf just laughed as he stared at me. He ignored my question and continued talking, "I had been in it the longest. I wanted to fight, to finish it, and here I was standing on the off ramp with a shotgun in my hands, with nothing to shoot at, watching cars pass me. The last car in the entourage was Deputy Jordan. He picked up Chisolm and me, and we were back in the chase. We were now the absolute last car. I felt some sorrow that I was going to miss out on the fight. I had stayed in the fight the longest, it was my fight… it was mine! There's this saying in police work, and it relates to fishing or hunting: 'If you catch them you clean them.'

"I felt safer now that I was in the rear, but at the same time, it saddened me. The road going north on Sierra Highway goes into the San Bernardino National Forest. It is a mixture of scrub and pine trees. This road led to Lytle Creek, which at the time was a shooting area. As we were driving, I was looking for someone with a rifle. I thought if I could just get a rifle I could fight these guys. We ended up driving on this dirt road about ten miles. On the way, we came upon a guy with a .30-06. I told him, 'Give me your gun, we have a cop killer on the loose.'

"He said, 'I'm sorry guys, I shot all my ammo.'

"Ah fuck. It was a heartbreaker. So, we just drove on. I'm still thinking fight, fight, fight. We came upon this old guy who had a lever action rifle. I was thinking all right, we got a 30-30. He gave me his rifle. I asked him if he had any ammo…and he hands me the ammunition, .22 caliber bullets."

Rolf looked down at his open hand as if he were holding little bullets and laughed.

"Oh well,' I thought, that's what we got, and up the hill we drove. I pulled this tube out of the rifle. It's where the bullets went into. So I have a handful of bullets, and I start loading the bullets into the tube. Some bullets are going in, some are falling on the floor. I couldn't even get the bullets in the tube with the car bouncing all over this dirt road. We got to the end of the road, where all the other cars were stopped, and as soon as we got out, I heard, **'I'M HIT!'** followed by a volley of shots. The bullets were firing so fast it sounded like one bullet. The shots were faster than a machine gun. It sounded like we were in a war zone with a hundred people firing as fast as they could. We were in this horseshoe shaped box canyon where rapid fire was echoing in with the actual firing. Deputy Evans had been the first car behind the suspects going up the road. At this time his car was out of my view. The shooting went on for about ten seconds. After the shooting ended, I was sort of walking around looking for a shot at the suspects. Then I saw them through the heavy brush and trees up the hill. I got down on one knee and took a shot at them. Then they disappeared. I was moving around left and right, looking for another shot. I would get a glimpse of them, then they would disappear again. It's unfortunate I never saw them again until court. That's how it ended for me."

"Oh, there's more?"

"Yes, there is. I meant that's how it ended with the suspects. I felt great sorrow and depression. I was fucking mad and sad for myself. I was not going to get a piece of their ass. There was a steep valley to go up and down to get to them. I wanted to go. I was asking guys to go with me. I was asking guys to cover us as we went up the hill after them. I had no takers. I then learned Deputy Evans was dead. He had been the first car in the procession going up Sierra Road, right behind the suspects. Every time he rounded a corner they just unloaded on him. He was able to crawl to the rear of his unit and fire back, but when he popped his head up to shoot again, they shot him in the head and killed him.

"He was a Vietnam veteran, and he was ready to go. Ready to fight, and they killed him."

Rolf was grim as he said this, his voice low.

"As I was trying to get guys to go up with me to get the suspects, I saw two guys escorting San Bernardino Deputy McCarty down the road toward me. That's when everybody noticed I had been shot. A helicopter had landed nearby. The assistant Sheriff from San Bernardino County was on scene, and he was telling me I needed to get on the helicopter and go to the hospital. I didn't want to go. I wanted to stay and fight.

"I actually contemplated going after the guys alone with my 22 rifle. I finally gave up my rifle, but only after my friend, another deputy assured me he was going to go after the suspects. Of course he didn't.

"McCarty and I got on the helicopter, and we lifted off. On the ride to the hospital, I found out more of the story. When the chase moved onto Sierra Highway after my car broke down, McCarty ended up being second in the procession, right behind Evans. As they were chasing the suspects up the road, anytime there was a curve where they lost sight of them, the suspects would stop and wait for them to come into view. As soon as they rounded the curve and came into view, they would open up on Evans. This happened all the way up the mountain. Remember I said we went up about ten miles? Right after Evans got shot, the suspects opened up on Deputy McCarty and McPherron who were in a radio car behind Evans. The suspects were walking down the hill in a line and just firing in unison. McPherron got out of the driver's door and ran to the back of his unit. McCarty crawled to the driver's side and also got out of the driver's door. Their fire was so intense, McCarty crawled under the car and tried to dig a hole in the dirt with his hands. McCarty had an automatic rifle he had taken from the evidence room at the station. From under his police car, he saw Evans in front of him at the rear of his own patrol car. He saw Evans reload his revolver, rise up to shoot and saw him collapse after he was shot in the head. This enraged him, and he crawled out from under his car and opened up on the suspects with the rifle, on fully automatic. When McCarty was shooting, he was raising his arms over the top of the hood of his unit, keeping his head down and blindly spraying bullets up towards the suspects. When he had his arms raised, one of the suspects shot him in the arm. But by shooting the automatic rifle, he backed the suspects up the hill, and caused them to stop firing. That was all the shooting I heard when I arrived at the scene. This was the sound of war. I was told some weeks later the suspects were actually walking down the hill with the intent of shooting all the cops they could. They knew they were winning the fight even though they had been running from us the entire time. It was McCarty shooting that M-16 that stopped their progress cold and turned them around.

"Prior to me landing at the hospital, Sheriff radio traffic in Lytle Creek notified Riverside dispatch that I had been shot in the head. One of our dispatchers called my wife and told her I'd been shot in the head and I was being flown to the hospital.

"Now I was safe. McCarty had been telling me his story. The adrenaline was no longer flowing. I was thinking about Evans being shot and how it had happened, and I became overwhelmed with emotions. I walked in the hospital. Everyone, all our personnel were committed to other things. I became a little light-headed, and wobbly legged. I got to the counter, and I told the personnel there, 'I gotta call my wife.' I'm so far from home; no one knows what's going on. I know this is big enough it is going to make the local if not national news. My wife knows me, and with something like this I'm going to be in the middle of it. When I called her she told me she had just gotten off the phone and had been told I'd been shot in the head. I told her, 'Yeah, but I'm okay… Jim Evans… he didn't make it.' I immediately started bawling my eyes out. Just bawling my eyes out. I pressed my back up against the wall and I was uncontrollably sobbing. I felt alone. McCarty had been wheeled out to the emergency room. All these strangers were staring at me crying. I felt deep, deep sorrow and an overwhelming feeling of being alone. I believed other people were dead, I just didn't know who or how many. I pulled myself together as I realized everyone was looking at me. No one had a clue what I had just gone through for the last ninety minutes. My wife wanted to come to the hospital, I told her not to. I hung up, and the nurses got me to a gurney. The doctor was looking at my head and ordering x-rays. All of a sudden, I got a tremendous pain in my right eye. I was screaming, 'My eye, my eye, something is in my eye!' People are looking at me weird, like he was okay a second ago, now he's in uncontrollable pain? The doctor got a black light device, put some dye in my eye and had a look. He said, 'Oh you got glass in your eye.' The doctor got some tools and plucked out a piece of glass oh about that big."

Rolf put his thumb and forefinger together, then brought his other index finger to the end where the two fingers met. It was maybe two millimeters long. "Rolf, that's a big piece of glass to be in your eye and not feel it for over an hour."

"It had been scratching my eye for two hours. I never felt it. Sometimes with the adrenaline, I think you could be dying and not feel a thing, others might, it depends on your body and your pain threshold.

"A lot of people from the rank of sergeant on up kept coming to see me. I had to tell the story to a lot of different people at the hospital. When they moved me to x-ray, I thought of Evans, and I started getting misty eyed again.

"Robert, it is important for people to know Evans hit one of the guys with a round of his 38 revolver. These guys were calm, cool, and collected. They knew what they were doing and planned on killing as many cops as they could before being killed themselves. Through the whole incident, they were tactically luring in the deputies. They did this by slowing down and letting the deputies catch up to them. Or perhaps, they stopped shooting to make the deputies believe they were out of ammunition.

Another thing they did was after turning a curve they would stop and wait for the deputies to round the same curve. As soon as they got in view, they just laid down a barrage of withering fire on them.

"All the cops at the scene hunkered down where they were. This was on the side of Mount Baldy. It got down to freezing that night. The suspects were in the hills, in the brush.

"The next morning, the Assistant Sheriff of the San Bernardino Sheriff's Department along with several other deputies drove to the command post. As they were driving up the mountain, they encountered two of the suspects, who were shivering from the cold. They willingly gave up without a struggle. One of the suspects had three handguns on him when they were arrested. The other had a gunshot wound to his back. It was determined it was Deputy Evans who shot him with one of his initial six shots before he was killed. A third suspect gave himself up when San Bernardino Sheriff's Deputies neared his hiding place. He had been shot twice. Both of these suspects survived. The Los Angeles County Sheriff's Department, Special Enforcement Bureau (S.E.B., the name for the Sheriff's Swat Team) was on scene the next day. They fielded 62 deputies. A helicopter saw the last suspect crouched in some bushes and directed the deputies to the location.

When two of the deputies arrived, the suspect pointed a revolver at them, and the S.E.B. deputies shot and killed him.

"So, they started the bank robbery with five suspects. One was shot and killed at the scene by Bolasky. Two others were shot. One by Evans, and another was killed by the Los Angeles County Sheriff's Department Special Enforcement Bureau. Forty-four felony counts were filed against all three surviving suspects, including the special circumstance murder of Deputy Evans. They all received life sentences without the possibility of parole. Here's what is really upsetting, Robert. When they were empaneling the jury (this is where the jury is selected by means of questions posed to them), two of the jurists stated under no circumstances would they vote for the death penalty. Over strenuous objections from the district attorney, the judge allowed these two jury members to remain. When the sentencing verdict of the trial came out, guess what? Two of the jury members voted to not impose the death penalty. It's maddening. One deputy died as a result of their actions. Two suspects killed. Eight people were wounded, and 33 police cars were damaged or put out of commission. There was a San Bernardino Sheriff helicopter that had come on scene during the chase at the 15 Freeway north of the 60 Freeway. The suspects shot it and set the flight instrument panel on fire, forcing the helicopter to land. So, one police helicopter was shot down, and numerous civilians were shot at. Some were hit, including a 12-year-old little boy. Houses were shot at, I guess just for fun. Civilian cars were shot at just because they were on the road driving. They had shot at me for 45 minutes. No death penalty. Maddening!!!

"Here's the story, the part of the story we found out after the detectives conducted their investigation. All suspects had records for minor drug charges. These guys were anarchists, survivalists, anti-government. They had made their bombs from instructions from a book about anarchy. They planned on exploding a gas main on one side of town, drawing all the deputies to that location far from the bank, while simultaneously robbing the bank. They had over two thousand rounds of ammunition, numerous homemade bombs, and incendiary devices. They stole the blue van that was used in the robbery. They had kidnapped the owner of the van so he could not call the police. He was tied up in the back of the van during the initial exchange of gunfire at the bank. At the edge of town, they had two cars that were clean, not stolen. They were going to dump the van and drive off in the cars. Who knows where they were going after that?

"Some good things came about after the shooting. It was slow in coming, but it did happen as a direct result of what occurred in this bank robbery. After months and years and a changing of the sheriff, the Riverside County Sheriff's Department's equipment was updated. They got a S.W.A.T. team. The communications system was updated. They got an aero bureau. They got a bomb disposal unit. There was a time during this event that had the San Bernardino Sheriff's helicopter not been on scene we would not have known where the suspects were. At the time we had no bomb or arson explosive unit. All this came later, but after the robbery, the Sheriff was getting so much heat for not keeping up with the times he balked. I feel as a result of much criticism, he became fed up. He gave no recognition or awards for any acts any of the men did or performed on this event. He didn't even honor Evans. I made a videocassette of the incident in 1982. It was eighteen years later in 2000, I transferred the cassette to a DVD. It was then the Riverside County Sheriff's Association and others approached me. They realized it was wrong how the men on that day had not been recognized. The present Sheriff said the Sheriff at the time of the shooting, had made his decision in this regard and he would not overturn that decision. After much press, he buckled. He awarded Jim Evans the Medal of Valor posthumously. Deputy Hille, Deputy Bolasky, Deputy Delgado and myself received the Medal of Courage, the next highest award. This award could be equated to the Silver Star in the military. Bolasky, Reed, Brown and I got the Gold Heart for being wounded in combat, equal to the Purple Heart in the military. This happened in 2000. Twenty years after the shooting. A side note is probably most departments would have given everybody the Medal of Valor. I think something should be said about this. I think it is incumbent upon leaders of sheriffs and police departments to properly recognize people for their courage and heroic acts. By not doing so minimizes their lives and the blood they've shed as not worthy of being recognized. By not doing so you are telling the person they should just be happy and lucky they have a job. I don't think those type of tough guy mentalities serve a place in modern society. It leaves a bad taste in people's mouths."

"Yes, it does."

"The California Highway Patrol Officers were awarded medals. The San Bernardino Deputies were awarded medals. We were not. Not until twenty years later. Go figure."

"Rolf, I did get an award. It was five years after my shooting. During this five-year period, the department instituted a new policy that deputies would wear a seatbelt until they were near the time they would be exiting their vehicles. Well, one of our deputies got in an accident and broke her arm. She got a medal for wearing her seatbelt. I never said anything to anyone. I never asked for any recognition, but when that happened, it put a bad taste in my mouth. I retired in May 1996. I got a call from my former detective lieutenant. We used to have a weekly detective meeting, and he invited me to that week's meeting. It was weird because I was already retired. I did not know why I was invited. At the end of the meeting, he presented me with a 'Meritorious Service Award' for saving my life and my partner's life on June 6, 1991. I got the award in August 1996. I later found out 'The Meritorious Service Award' is normally given to those who make great administrative contributions and changes to the department. The award does not match in any way shape or form what my partner and I went through. The timing of them giving me the award was, at least to me, almost like an afterthought. I love the Los Angeles County Sheriff's Department, but sometimes it gets confusing."

"Robert, I sometimes wonder if people know or care about what we do? Do they care that we risk our lives? When I was at the hospital on the gurney, a guy down the hallway must've seen me crying in uniform. He shouted out to me, 'God bless you, man!' Robert, sometimes it's a guy on a gurney that tells you they appreciate you."

*****

The fact is that five guys committed a take-over robbery of a bank using heavy assault rifles and it had a major impact on law enforcement for many years. This was highly unusual for 1980. TV broadcasters described the robbery and pursuit in terms of being a "Bonnie & Clyde" type robbery. It had been decades since any crime close to this nature and magnitude had been committed. It was in fact, the first of its kind in terms of length of time the shooting went on, and the number of bullets fired. It occurred long before the North Hollywood Bank Robbery that made national fame in 1997. The Norco Bank Robbery positively changed how police responded to these kinds of incidents and was the basis for improving police radios, the forming of SWAT teams, the forming of Bomb Squads, and the forming of helicopter units to conduct pursuits.

For the reader, the DVD that Rolf made has been uploaded to You-Tube by persons unknown to him. It is in three parts and can be viewed by those interested. It's as interesting today as it was then, as there are much more people today using assault rifles and sometimes explosives to commit crimes or terrorism (example the Boston Marathon and the days that followed). The DVD includes portions of the actual radio transmissions depicting the deputies' broadcasts after being shot and while in pursuit. It also has actual crime scene photos and a professional narrator. You will feel like Rolf did when he was in the radio car on that fateful day of May 9, 1980.

Here was the ending tally as a result of that day:

- Jim Evans killed.

- 33 police units damaged or destroyed by gunfire, explosives, or collisions.

- One police helicopter forced to land when their radio was shot and caused an electrical fire.

- 8 Deputies & California Highway Patrol Officers shot.

- The landing path beneath the Ontario Airport was disrupted while the pursuit traveled beneath it.

- Handmade hand grenades (IEDs) were brought, and three were thrown.

- Hand thrown Molotov cocktails were brought, (but not used). They had been designed from instructions in the Anarchist Cookbook.

- Thousands of rounds of ammunition were brought with hundreds if not thousands of rounds fired at law enforcement.

- Four deputies involved in this incident would retire from service within a few months after the event.

*****

Rolf Parkes received the Riverside Gold Heart from the Riverside County Sheriff's Department for being wounded on the afternoon of May 9, 1980.

Rolf Parkes also received the Medal of Courage from the Riverside County Sheriff's Department for his actions on the afternoon of May 9, 1980. It is the second highest award the department can bestow upon its sworn deputies.

He received these awards in 2000. Twenty years after the incident.

Chapter 9

The Jungle

Ursula Ave. and Tacana St., Los Angeles, CA

My boss told me as much of Richard's story as he knew, but it was very sparse. He said after Richard was shot, he refused to sit or lay down because he was afraid if he did he would die. It was enough to send chills down my spine and rivet my interest.

I got a hold of Richard and we spoke on the phone. It turned out we had briefly worked together after he and I were retired. But neither of us remembered each other. Still, there was no doubt we worked together, the months we worked at the location were right. I sent him a copy of the beginning of this book and my shooting, the first chapter. When we talked next he told me he would like to share his story.

Richard is such a nice man, a gentleman. "Robert, if this story only helps one person, one cop survive, I want to be a part of it." At the same time he is a gentleman, you get the sense he is a no-nonsense kind of guy. A tough guy who you would not want to cross. I was slightly reminded of a Dragnet type guy, (A 1960's television show featuring an unemotional L.A.P.D. detective), who gave the facts and nothing but the facts. It turned out he was a very close friend with George Barthel who was a Los Angeles County Deputy Sheriff who had been killed on the job. George Barthel was shot to death on April 19, 1979. The reason I mention this is Richard brought it up right after he learned I had been on the Los Angeles County Sheriff's Department. He asked if I had known George. I hadn't. It was very evident that George's death still bothered Richard very much. He told me, "We were best friends."

It's interesting how many different people I've met over the years felt the same way. George must have been quite an impressive person. I never met him but I'm sure I missed something important. Why? The many people I've met throughout my life who knew George have told me he was the consummate cop. He was always trying to improve tactics throughout the department. But what comes through more than anything, what I keep hearing, is he genuinely cared about people. Like Richard.

To hear a real cop like Richard praise Deputy Barthel, and to see the pain in his eyes so many years later over George's death, told me worlds about George Barthel's character and the respect he engendered amongst other men.

*****

"I joined L.A.P.D. in 1969. I had just gotten out of Recon, (the Marine Corps Special Forces), with the United States Marine Corps. I was just out of Vietnam. Three years later in 1972, I was working morning watch (eleven at night to seven in the morning) at Wilshire Division. In December of that year, I had made training officer. I was assigned a probationer named Jack. My job was to teach him about police work and procedures, how to handle a radio car. He was a sharp guy. He picked up things quickly, and he had made some great observations regarding people involved with suspicious activity and he was doing great for a guy new to patrol.

"Let me tell you about my schedule the day before the incident took place. I had worked the shift before, from eleven at night to seven in the morning. When I got off shift at seven, I had to be in court and was in court all day long. I got out of court about four p.m. and then drove about 40 miles home. I got home knowing I had to be back at work at about 10:30 or so to get ready for my next shift. It was going to be Jack's first night driving. I was exhausted and I was very short of sleep. I knew I would have a long day ahead of me and I was glad Jack was driving.

"It was January 31, 1973. We were patrolling the south end of Wilshire Division. We drove into the Jungle, and we saw a 1969 black Cadillac El Dorado. (This is an area of apartment complexes that have a lot of shrubbery and palm trees and is called the Jungle because of the amount of shrubbery in the complex. It is generally and loosely bordered by La Brea Avenue on the west, Stocker Street on the east, and Santa Rosalia Drive and Coliseum on the north). We were westbound on Pinafore Street stopped at a stop sign at Ursula Avenue when we first saw the Cadillac. It was traveling northbound on Ursula and was stopped at the stop sign to our left. As you know, we take notice of things, and I saw there was no front license plate on the car and there were four people inside. We were driving in an area known for high drug activity where a lot of drug transactions took place. It was two in the morning. In that era, Cadillacs were being stolen all the time. There were no other cars out. It was just the two of us, the Cadillac and us. I told Jack, 'Let the vehicle go by.' I wanted to get behind the car. I was now in the observation mode. We let the Cadillac continue north on Ursula. It passed in front of us while we were stopped at the stop sign. We made a right turn and slid in behind them. When the car passed us, I ran the license plate. I decided to stop the car, at least until the return (the results) came back on the plate. We were now on Ursula Ave. just before Tacana Street.

"We initiated a stop as we were driving north on Ursula Ave. They stopped on Ursula right before the street turned and became Tacana. When we stopped, I told Jack, 'Be careful, get the driver out of the car and pat him down. (Patting down someone means to feel over their clothes for any possible weapon. Folks, so you get it when you have someone you are training you do not assume anything. You explain exactly what you want them to do).

"Robert, when Jack got the driver out of the car it was immediate. This guy was very verbally belligerent, and a little jumpy, although he did comply with the pat down. 'Why are you stopping me?' He said, 'What did I do wrong? What are you doing? You can't do this. You're stopping me because I'm a nigger!' I could hear all of this. I was behind the passenger door of our police car watching the occupants of the car and the actions of the suspect. When the license plate information returned, we were informed there were three misdemeanor warrants associated with the license plate.

"There was a female passenger in the middle of the front seat, a male passenger was sitting next to her in the right front seat, and a male passenger was in the backseat. It was a two-door car. Jack had retrieved the driver license from the driver. He and the driver were now between the rear of their car and the front of our radio car. I came up and got the driver license from Jack. I needed the driver license to compare the information on it with the information returned from running the license plate. I wanted to see if it matched anything the dispatcher told us about the car. The driver was still belligerent with Jack. About a minute and a half had gone by. I walked back to my car, and I heard another radio car in the north end of the division request assistance because of a possible burglary suspect. We had six cars out, six cars throughout the division. Although the driver was verbally challenging, I thought the other unit requesting assistance needed help more than me. I held off asking for backup, although I was thinking I might need it. The driver's name did not match any of the warrants associated with the car. I had already run the plate, but now I ran his name. His name came back as 'no want, no warrant.' He had no warrants. I wanted to know about the car. I wanted to know about the misdemeanor warrants associated with the car, who the people with the warrants were. Maybe they were in the car. Maybe it was the owner of the car. I wanted to know who owned the car since the driver's name did not come back when we ran the plate. Things were not adding up. If you add all the above with the driver's attitude, it was suspicious. Usually, when you aren't doing anything wrong, you give your driver license and registration and get on with your day. If he had not been acting like he was, it would have been exactly that: 'Thank you for your cooperation, have a nice evening.' My suspicions would not have been so aroused. It seemed like he was trying to divert our attention from something.

"My partner and this driver are still between our two cars. The driver was still argumentative. The people in the car were rubbernecking, looking behind them to see what was going on. I approached the driver, 'Is this your car?'

"He answered me, 'You don't believe a nigger can own a Cadillac?' and he went on and on in that similar type of talk. He was very belligerent and disrespectful.

"I thought it was off for him to answer with a statement like that when I had asked a simple question. I went up to the front driver's windshield to look at the V.I.N. (Vehicle Identification Number).

"I went back to the driver, 'All I want to do is verify this car is yours.'

"He answered, and I remember exactly what he said, 'The motherfucking papers are inside the glove box!!!'

"I said in a calm tone, 'That's what we're going to do. We're just going to verify the car is yours.'

"So, I walked to the front of the passenger side of the car and started getting everyone out. As you know from an officer's safety point of view, you do not go into a car with people sitting inside. So, one at a time I got the people out. The front male passenger was the first guy I got out. He was the brother of the driver. His driver license was now clipped to my tie clip. I then got the male from the rear passenger seat out of the car. After patting him down, I clipped his identification to my tie. At this time the driver was at the trunk of the Cadillac, his brother was standing at the center of the trunk, and the rear passenger was standing at the right side of the trunk. Their hands were on the trunk. My partner was behind and to the left of all three men. The female was still in the car. As you know, it's tough to watch everyone. I had a lot of people to watch, and while I was taking the men out of the car, I had been watching the female. She was extremely nervous. She was picking up her purse and then putting it back down. Picking it up, and putting it down. As she was doing this, she kept looking back through the rear window toward the driver. From the way she was looking, I got the feeling she was trying to get a sign from the driver as to what she should do."

Richard described the female to me in vivid detail. It seemed he remembered every detail of this event perfectly.

"The female was half black and half American Indian. She had straight black hair. She was wearing a black dress and was a little overweight. I told her, 'Okay slide on out.' I was looking at the guys at the rear of the trunk, I was looking at her. I was busy.

"When I told the woman to get out of the car, the driver said, **'BITCH STAY IN THE CAR!!! YOU'RE NOT GETTING OUT!!!'** and he said it several times. She was still in the car and looking over at the driver, undecided on what to do.

"I ordered her, 'GET OUT OF THE CAR!' and she started to comply. She had her purse in her hand, and I was looking at it because of the nervous way she had been picking it up and putting it down. I didn't know what was in it. When she started to get out of the car, the driver pushed his way in front of the other two men, shoving them off of the trunk of the Cadillac and headed toward the female as if to block her from getting out of the car. He was now to my left and in front of the open car door. Things were now getting out of control. The driver had just broken away very quickly from my partner's control and was now dictating what was going to happen, taking control of the stop.

"I got him in an upper body control hold. I got my right arm around his neck, and I was trying to render him unconscious. I need to describe the clothes he was wearing so you understand what happened next. Robert, this was in 1973 they were all dressed up like Superfly. (I realize some of you might not know what I'm talking about. Just look it up on the internet). The driver was wearing a huge pimp Superfly hat, a huge thick fur collar, three-quarter length blue crushed velvet coat, and platform shoes. The driver was thirty-five years old, six feet three inches tall and about two hundred and thirty pounds.

"After I got my arm around his neck I was immediately able to get him to the ground in a seated position. I was kneeling behind him with my arm around his neck. The female is still sitting in the car watching all of this. I wanted to handcuff this guy, but I couldn't choke him out, I couldn't render him unconscious because of his big fur collar. Adding to his fur collar, you have to remember it was two thirty in the morning in January. It was cold outside, and I was wearing a big Milton police jacket. We were struggling, but no problem, I was in control, I had the guy. I yelled, 'Jack get over here.' Jack came over and grabbed the driver's right arm. The other two guys stayed at the trunk of the car. They were just watching. I tried to get his other arm behind him to get him handcuffed, and I couldn't get the handcuffs on him. He was really struggling around and I just couldn't get them on.

"The driver yells out, **'BROTHERS HELP ME, HELP ME!'** The other two guys left the trunk of the Cadillac and came over to where Jack and I were on the ground struggling with the driver. I could see they were thinking of jumping in the fight. Things are happening in fractions of a second now. Things slowed down. Everything was slow motion. My adrenaline was coursing through my body. I told my partner, 'Jack, get on the radio.' I didn't want to say anything more. I didn't want them to hear we needed help.

"In my vision, Jack slowly got up, and as he went for the radio car, the two guys who had been at the trunk of the Cadillac intercepted him, and stopped him. I saw all this as I was struggling on the ground. Jack had his baton out.

"As we were struggling the driver asked me, 'What are you doing?'

"You're under arrest!" I answered.

"He said, 'I'll make you have to kill me!' As he was saying this, I could feel him pulling on my holstered gun. I knew I was in a life-threatening situation. It was life and death. We were outnumbered. I had my hands full. Jack had his hands full. The driver was trying to get my gun. I was really scared, scared out of my mind but still, I was thinking and fighting.

"I broke the driver's grip. I got his hand off of my gun, and I now had it out of the holster. Things were moving so slowly each event seemed to take minutes, not milliseconds. Understand we are rolling all over the ground at this time. Fighting. Somehow in all the rolling and elbowing and hitting, he got behind me. We were on the ground, and he wrapped both of his hands around either side of my body, like a hug, and he was holding onto my gun, which I had in a two-handed grip in front of me.

"As we were struggling we moved from being on the ground to standing. Next, we would be on the ground again rolling violently. In the next instant, we would be on our feet fighting, banging against different parked cars, both of us hanging onto the gun. As all this was going on, I was trying to get in a position to shoot the driver.

"I was trying to shoot the driver, but I didn't have control of the gun. I tried to pull the trigger, and it wouldn't budge! I couldn't pull the trigger. He had a grip wrapped around the cylinder and frame of the gun, thereby cementing them together. (On a revolver the cylinder has to turn to fire. If you hold the cylinder and frame together at the same time, the cylinder will not turn, and you cannot pull the trigger and the gun will not fire). Things were desperate. I had to get his hands off of my gun. I had to get to where I could shoot him. I bent forward and bit one of his hands as hard as I could. I was enraged, absolutely enraged. He let go of the gun with that one hand but was still holding onto the gun with the other hand. When I got his hand off of the gun, he shoved his fingers into my right eye and tried to pull my eye out. Instinctively, and in excruciating pain, I let go of my gun with my left hand and jerked my head violently backward and to the side, while I simultaneously pulled his fingers out of my eye with my left hand. While doing this, I was still conscious. I had to hang onto my gun. He had already told me I was going to have to kill him. He was yelling at me, '**I'M GOING TO KILL YOU, YOU FUCKING PIG!! I'M GOING TO KILL YOU!!!**' I had no doubt he wanted to kill me and was trying to do just that. I was scared. This was a life and death struggle I was in, but I wanted to live. We had been fighting for about a minute and a half." (Time it, folks. Then imagine fighting all out for your life for that period of time).

"Now we were on the ground again. We had moved toward the curb as the fight had continued. We were several cars away from the radio car by now. I was on the ground with my feet toward the curb and my head sort of under a parked car. I scooted under the car as much as I could. I was facing the rear of the car. The driver was behind me holding onto my gun from behind. I then pushed my arm forward right against the front bumper of the car and was finally able to break his grip on my gun.

"He yells, **'GET THE BITCH OUT OF THE CAR WITH THE GUN, GET THE BITCH OUT OF THE CAR WITH THE GUN!!!'**

"I was wondering if there was someone else around I didn't know about. I was wondering who he was yelling at. I was so focused on surviving I really didn't have a lot of time to wonder about Jack. What I didn't know was Jack had made it to the radio car and had put out a call for help, but as he was doing so, the brother of the driver had pulled Jack's baton from his hands. Jack tried to get his baton back, and they had their own struggle going on. Jack eventually lost the struggle for the baton and the brother was unmercifully hitting Jack over the head and was driving Jack down to the ground between the driver's door and the radio car.

"I was thinking I had to get out from under this car. I was thinking she was going to come up and shoot me in the head. I rolled out from under the car, and again the driver and I were fighting over my gun. We were rolling on the ground. The driver was behind me and we were on our backs. I looked up, and the female was standing over me. The driver yelled, **'KILL THAT FUCKING PIG, KILL THAT FUCKING PIG!!!'** So slowly, I can see it now, so slowly she reached into her bra. I was kicking at her, violently, and as I did so, she would jump back. I was kicking at her desperately, but my legs couldn't reach her. The driver was holding me from behind. He was yelling at her, **BITCH**

KILL THAT FUCKING PIG!' She pulled a gun out from her bra, and so very slowly in such a slow and deliberate motion pointed it at my chest. As she was moving her hand and pointing it at me, it was like frame… frame… frame… frame. I knew she was going to shoot me. I was thinking, 'I've got to survive this for my son.' I started rolling as violently as I could. I was hoping she would miss me and shoot the driver. I wanted to take him with me. I figured if she shot him, I could get my gun and then kill them both. That's what I was really hoping for. That's when I saw the muzzle flash of her gun and heard two pops. She shot me two times in the chest. I couldn't believe it… But I was still going, still fighting. The shots felt like two stings. I thought, 'Is that all there is? Is that what it's like to get shot?'

"I later found out she had shot me with a .22 caliber revolver.

"The driver could see I was still full of fight. He yelled out, **'HELP US, HELP US!'** One of the males came over and grabbed my legs. He held my legs, as the driver held my upper torso. This stretched my torso out and severely hampered me from rolling around and fighting. The woman then stuck the gun in the center of my stomach. I tried to kick her, but my legs were pinned. I screamed at the woman, **'DON'T DO IT, DON'T DO IT!!!'** Again, I thought of my son. I thought, 'I have to be here for him. He needs me.' He was only one year old and he had his whole life ahead of him. I couldn't bear the thought of him living without me. I saw the determination in the face of the woman. She fired. I lost track of time then. I blacked out. I blacked out when she shot me, and I have no idea why. I guess it was because of the impact of the shot to my stomach, but I don't know. I have no idea if it was a millisecond, a second or several seconds, but when I was back, I realized my gun was no longer in my hands. I had no backup gun. We were still on our backs, with me lying face up on top of him. The driver was now pushing me off of him. I was thinking he now had my gun. My mind was screaming at me, **I'VE GOT TO GET MY GUN!** I jumped up and reached down to my waist. My baton was still there. Our fight was so violent I could not believe I still had my baton. In the midst of all the action, in the midst of having been shot three times, after blacking out, I had the thought it was incredulous that my baton had not fallen out of my baton ring. The driver was lying on the ground on his back, and he was pushing back with the heels of his feet, scooting, shimmying away from me. I saw he had my gun in his hand, but he was fumbling with it. He didn't have it in his hands properly where he could shoot. So, as he was scooting away, he was simultaneously and furiously trying to get my gun into his hand so he could shoot. The only way I now had to defend myself was with my baton, and I was swinging it as hard and as fast as I could. I was trying to knock the gun out of his hand. He was able to get just a little out my reach, and that's when I threw my baton at him and turned. I was running to dive behind a parked car. As I dove behind the car, he was shooting at me with my gun. I got shot for the fourth time in the left buttocks. That really hurt. By now I must have been a little dazed because I honestly didn't know how many times the driver shot me. It could have been five times. I thought it was. I didn't realize it was only one time. Things were happening in milliseconds but time seemed to drag on with each second feeling like a century.'

"I found out later while this was going on, Jack had his own life and death struggle unfolding. The brother had hit Jack on the head with his baton, and Jack got his gun out. The brother then grabbed Jack's gun, and they were fighting over it. Jack was close to me, but I never saw him. Jack later said he saw me getting shot, but he couldn't get to me, he was fighting for his own life.

"While Jack was fighting for his gun with the brother, and right after I dove behind the parked car, the driver rushed to Jack and pointed my gun at his stomach. He fired. Jack saw the driver aiming at his stomach, and while fighting the brother, Jack managed to turn sideways, just enough so the bullet missed him. This round went into the car door. The driver then stuck my gun into Jack's abdomen and fired into him. It was a contact shot (point blank). Jack went to the ground. I didn't see any of this because I was behind the parked car. Remember, this was happening in milliseconds.

"I heard them screaming, 'Let's get out of here!' Now the bullet wounds were catching up to me. It was getting hard to breathe. I poked my head out from around the parked car, and I could see multiple muzzle flashes, and I knew they were shooting at me. I ducked back not wanting to get shot again. I then heard tires screeching. As soon as I heard the tires screeching, I ran to Jack. He was lying in the street in a fetal position. I saw blood all over his head, and I said, 'Hang on, hang on.' I thought, 'Jack's been shot in the head.' I ran to the car. I wanted to get the shotgun out, but I couldn't get it out. I kept pulling on it, but I couldn't get it out. Something I had done hundreds of times before, and so easily, was now impossible. Then I thought, 'I've got to get help.' I looked for the microphone and couldn't find it. I found the radio and grabbed the microphone cord. Hand over hand I pulled the microphone cord knowing at the end was the microphone. When I got to the end of the cord, the microphone was missing. They had ripped it out.

"I went back to Jack, 'It's okay Jack, hang on.' I didn't want to sit down. I didn't want to move. Panic was rising inside me. I had just handled a shooting about a month before this incident. The victim had been a woman. She had been shot in the chest. When we got there, she had been having trouble breathing. When we laid her in the ambulance, she died; drowned to death in her own blood. I knew my lung or lungs were filling with blood and I was slowly drowning. Terror was at the edge of my mind. I consciously shoved the panic down forcing myself to relax, forcing myself to get every molecule of oxygen. I didn't want to expend any unnecessary energy, so that I would not use up any life-saving oxygen. I needed every molecule of it. I leaned against the trunk of the radio car with my feet on the ground. I was facing Jack. I was scared, on the edge of panic, but I knew I had to stay calm. I knew we were both hurt really bad. Jack was a mess of blood and still curled up in a fetal position. I was drowning. I thought we might both die.

"Neighbors had been calling the police about shots fired. Jack's broadcast for help went through, and I could hear sirens coming. Soon after that, other officers arrived. I gave them the description of the guys. If you remember, I had clipped the suspects' identifications to my tie clip.

They found the identifications lying on the ground. I told them I had just run the car, so they had that description.

"They found the rear passenger a couple of blocks away. It turned out he had not gotten into the car as it drove away. He had run from the scene of the shooting. When the officers approached him, he threw up his hands and said, 'I didn't have anything to do with the shooting of the police.' I think he was the guy who held my legs down when the female shot me in the stomach. Because I was mostly paying attention to the female while that part of the shooting went down, I could not positively identify him as the guy who pulled my legs.

"As our investigators moved on the case they were just about an hour behind the suspects and their movements. They got an address of an apartment on San Vicente Boulevard. They found the female shooter there. She had been dropped off about an hour before. They found her lying on the couch, and the gun she had shot me with was under the cushion. Our investigators then found out the two brothers had changed cars and got more guns. They were planning to drive to the Burbank Airport and hijack an airplane to Cuba.

"While this was going on, Jack and I were in the hospital. On the way, I could hardly breathe. They got me to California Hospital in downtown Los Angeles at Fourteenth and Hope Street and stuck a tube down my throat. I threw up. Then they slit my side open with a scalpel and shoved a tube into my chest. I saw the tube fill up with blood. It was the blood from my lung. Almost immediately I could breathe again. I had been drowning.

"While I had my fun, the investigators were gathering information. They found out that one of the guys was connected to an apartment in North Hollywood on Riverside Drive.

"The two brothers were there and had just left the apartment and were getting into their car in the alley. They saw a black and white radio car driving toward them. They were going to kill the officer, but then they saw a second black and white behind them. The two brothers threw their guns onto the floorboard, and got out of their car with their hands in the air and gave up.

"They think the driver was part of a bank robbery crew. They couldn't prove it. He had just gotten out of prison and was on parole for murder. He paid cash for the Cadillac. How in the world could he afford to pay cash for a Cadillac when he had just gotten out of prison?

"Before I got onto the operating table I was told all four suspects were in custody. When I got into recovery, I lifted up the sheet covering me and was horrified. I had flaps of skin sewed together all the way up my stomach. The lieutenant was there. I asked, 'Jack?' I was afraid to ask. He patted me on the arm, 'You did okay kid, you did okay. You're okay, and Jack is okay.' Both Jack and I were in the hospital for a whole month. I went home, and after a little while, I was going nuts. I had to get back to work. I spoke with the lieutenant. 'Please bring me back to work, but don't put me on the desk. I need to get back to the field.'

"I knew Jack was having some issues… I was having issues. But I still needed to get back to work. So, a month and a half later I went to work, and they put me on the desk. However, soon after that, I was back in the field."

*****

"The driver was on parole for murder. They filed assault with a deadly weapon on a police officer. I was thinking, 'Why not attempted murder on a police officer?' It didn't make sense to me. Well if you can believe this, assault with a deadly weapon had a much stiffer sentence than attempted murder on a police officer. His brother had done time for burglary. The female had done time for mayhem. When we got to court, and after he was found guilty, the judge took me into his chambers and told me, 'You'll never ever see this guy again. He's going to be put away forever.'"

*****

"About six or seven years later I was a Sergeant II. I was on loan to narcotics. I was partnered up with an old-time narcotics detective, Dick, who was teaching me the ropes. We went to the Saint Francis Hotel in Hollywood to investigate a complaint of narcotic activity. The hotel has a courtyard area surrounding the apartments. We went onto the roof and were looking down into the open curtains of some of the windows of the apartments facing the courtyard area. On the next story down was a man sitting on a table and he was separating weed. He was making joints. Dick said, 'Let's go knock on that door.'

"I said, 'Okay.' And down we went. We knocked on the door, and when they opened it, we were in. We had seen a felony occur and walked in when the door opened. It turned out there were two guys inside. I had one and Dick had the other. Immediately I knew the guy I had against the wall was the driver. The guy who fought me for my gun. The guy who told the female to shoot me. The guy who held me as the female shot me. The guy who took my gun and shot me. The guy who shot Jack. That guy. He was out, and I was again hand to hand with him. He didn't recognize me. I wasn't in uniform. I didn't tell him who I was. I was in shock. I pulled my gun and backed up. Dick knew something was wrong. I went to Dick and whispered, 'Dick, this is the guy who shot me.'

"Dick said, 'Don't worry they're both going to jail. They're both under the influence.' Both guys were handcuffed, but I was really uncomfortable. I wanted to kill this guy.

"'Dick, it's five stories down. I'm going to throw him over the courtyard.'

"Dick was worried, I mean if I killed this guy we're both going down. Again, he reassured me, 'Don't worry he's going to jail.'

"I knew I had to get control of myself and calm down, but I was having problems doing so. Finally, I thought of what I had to lose, and I talked myself out of killing him and decided to trust Dick.

"This guy had given me a bullshit identification. I mean I knew his name. We later learned the identification he was using was stolen in a robbery. That victim could not identify the suspect. I rode in the backseat with both of the suspects as we went back to the station. The guy knew something was wrong. Finally, he blurted out, 'I remember.'

"Dick, who was driving turned and said, 'What do you remember?'"

"He answered, 'I remember something I'm not proud of.' I took it to mean when I got shot.

"He got six months for being under the influence of a controlled substance, an opiate. He got nothing for having the robbery victim's identification because the victim couldn't identify him as the robbery suspect."

*****

"Six months later another call went out. It was at a hotel; a kidnapping in progress. I got there after most of the officers showed up. I walked in the room where the officers had about three or four guys detained, and there he was again. An instant later my gun was drawn on him. The officers did the right thing and got everyone handcuffed and under control. The word got out to the officers in the division. Everyone knew who he was. He couldn't even move without getting stopped.

"The station psychologist approached me one day.

"He asked me, 'How are you doing with all the stuff you're going through?'

"I told him, 'Yeah it's hard, but I'm okay.'

"He told me, 'Look, think about it this way. This guy is a hype. He is going to die with a needle in his arm. You have a lot to lose. He will get his.'

"He was right."

*****

We were each walking to our respective cars. The interview was over. We were chitchatting. "Richard, they don't teach you to bite people when you're fighting."

"Robert, when you are fighting for your life, when it's life and death, anything goes. All the rules go out of the window."

We kept walking and chitchatting. He was so nonchalant throughout the interview I had to comment. "Richard you're pretty calm about the story."

He then got a look on his face. Very serious, but with a very slight hint of a smile at the corner of his lips. His sunglasses were on, and I couldn't see his eyes, "Oh, it's always there, right below the surface." Another natural pause in our conversation happened as we walked. Richard said, "Now that we talked about it and I relived it, it will bother me a little later." He was about to go on but then hesitated. It was as if he didn't need to say what he was going to say. He smiled at me and said instead as we shook hands, "Well, you know."

*****

Oh, I almost forgot to tell you. I know you remember how Richard thought of his one-year-old son throughout his life and death fight, and his desire to be there for his son throughout his life. Well, he was. Richard had such a positive influence on his son that his son followed in his father's footsteps. He has been a deputy sheriff for the last fifteen years now, proudly and honorably serving the community. Last year the San Bernardino County Sheriff's Department singularly recognized Richard's son by bestowing upon him the distinguished "Safety Employee of the Year" award.

*****

Richard went on to have a fantastic career with the Los Angeles Police Department. He served as a member of the world-famous S.W.A.T.

team. He became a part of the Los Angeles Police Department's, "Aero Bureau," and flew helicopters supporting the ground units. He also lectured at the Los Angeles Police Department as an Academy Instructor where he has imparted many of his hands-on experiences to other new recruits. He has been teaching at the different academies since 1980. He has had some former recruits tell him years later that he really helped them get through some of the tough things they experienced.

Richard is very proud he has been able to do this.

I asked Richard if he received any recognition for his actions that night.

He looked at me, "They don't give you medals for getting shot."

Richard Beardslee is to be awarded the Los Angeles Police Department's "Purple Heart" in September 2014 for the severe, life-threatening injuries he sustained on January 31, 1973.

Chapter 10

Coke Partners

Florence Ave. and Compton Ave., Los Angeles, CA

Heroes. Have you defined them yet? I can't. To me it's confusing. None of these guys…, err, excuse me Stacy, and women, consider themselves heroes. If they are not, then who is? How about these next two guys, the wetbacks?

*****

Booker is a small black man with a heart of gold. He is a talker. Booker never met anyone he didn't know or like. It is next to impossible to have a conversation with Booker without his cell phone ringing. It's always some real estate deal or other deal that needs his immediate attention. He laughs all the time. What I admire about Booker is he is humble and quick to admit when he doesn't know something.

I was looking for coppers' (police officers') stories so I could finish this book and I was asking around. I had already asked Booker about three times if he knew anyone who had been shot. "Hey hey hey hey ah, hahahahaha," Booker said in a voice too deep for his little five-foot-five-inch body. "I just thought of somebody," he told me.

"Fuck Book, what the hell took you so long?" I was almost done with the book.

"Oh, hey, ah, ha, hahaha. I forgot about it. These two were the shot callers. Bad. Baaad dudes. Gunfighters, for real."

"Yeah Book. Look a lot of us were gunfighters. A lot of us were bad dudes. For real and true, not pretend bad dudes."

"Yeah Rango!" It's how he pronounces my name. "I know you are bad, you were the leader of the goon squad!" Another investigator walked by, "Hey hey hey hey." Booker stopped them. "Do you know Rango? He was bad, a real bad dude; ran the jail. He ran the goon squad. Every day they got on the radio. Every day they dogged me, 'Get it right Mister Probation Officer.'"

Booker was referring to when he and I worked the jails together in 1983, and people thought I was part of some supposed goon squad.

"Yeah Book, tell him why we used to say that."

Booker's voice raised three octaves, "I don't know." His voice got deeper, "Ah, hahaha. Look I came from probations, the county probation department." He was explaining this to the poor guy walking by. "Then I became a deputy. Man, these deputies were crazy. Tough, real rough and tough guys. They didn't like the way I talked on the radio." We all laughed, and the other investigator walked away.

"Book, do you have someone for my book or not?"

"Yeah, I forgot, Rango. When I got to Century, they were the shot callers."

"Booker, what do you mean?"

"Rango, they were ghetto cops. Smart, tough, respected, they knew the streets, and they knew what they were doing. Man, these dudes had been in numerous shootings. Seriously Rango, when I made sergeant I didn't want to go to Century. Guys were getting five to eight calls at a time of shootings every night. Man, I had been working backgrounds ten years. I didn't know the streets anymore, I was 50 years old. Too old to be working patrol, much less Century. Angel took me under his wings and helped me. He protected me. I have nothing but respect for him. Without him, I don't know what I would have done."

*****

I emailed Angel. A few days later he emailed me back, and I called him. Oh, I liked him right away. This was a cop. The kind of tough cop I liked working with.

He told me right away he was interested in telling his story, but he wasn't so sure about Javier. I found out where Javier was working and was able to get a hold of him several days later. Javier told me he couldn't talk and would call me the next day. The next day came and went. No call from Javier. About a week later I tracked Javier down again. He told me he had been sick with a sore throat and couldn't talk. I didn't quite believe him. So far only one person I had approached declined to tell his story. I thought Javier was going be the second. After I told him how these stories the storytellers were sharing were keeping me up at night and giving me stomachaches, he told me I could email him my story. Then I got a hint of the truth. He said he didn't like talking about the incident. Two days later after reading my story, he told me he would like to share his, that it was worth talking about if he could help another officer survive.

When I interviewed him and got his story, I found out why he didn't like talking about it.

Horrific.

*****

Javier and his wife are some of the most hospitable people I've ever met.

"Robert, come to my house we can do the interview in the backyard." It was the first interview I had done at someone's house.

Javier brought out some water. His wife later came out and lightly berated him for not offering me food. She had a tray of fresh strawberries, and home baked chocolate chip cookies. It was easy to see how he had made a great family life with her.

Soft-spoken and humble, one would wonder about Booker's description of this man as a bad dude...

"I was born in Mexico, Jalisco, in a little village. We had very humble beginnings. My parents emigrated here when I was young. I came to the United States when I was about seven. My parents were chasing the American Dream. We were poor, really poor. I grew up in Huntington Park, South Gate, Bell, and Downey. It was tough in the beginning. There were seven of us kids, and we lived in a two-bedroom apartment. Then there were my two parents, and we had my grandfather here also. That's ten-people living in a two-bedroom apartment. My dad worked making mattresses, he did some carpentry work, you know working for minimum wages. He just worked all the time. My mom worked in the sweatshops, sewing for minimum wages. We managed to get by without any government assistance whatsoever. We never asked for money, there was none. All we got was food, shelter, and clothing. As we got older, we started working and helping out with money. The only time I got in trouble was when my brother made some nunchuks (a martial arts weapon with two pieces of wood connected with a chain or cord). I was in front of my home and was playing around with them. I was about 15. The cops arrested me and told me it was a felony to have them. I didn't know. They probably thought I was a gang member. But I wasn't. None of my brothers or sisters ever got in trouble. My older brothers and sisters were working two jobs to make money and help out the family so we could survive. My older sister and brother actually dropped out of high school to get two jobs to help out the family. They had to finish high school at night school. Growing up I was a paperboy. I worked at a meat market waiting on customers, and when I was in high school, I worked at a gas station as a cashier part-time.

"In the late seventies, we got our legal residency here in the United States. That's when I became a United States citizen. I got married young. I was 20. Most of my brothers and sisters got married young also. It was still tough. I was working for Smart and Final. My wife then got a fulltime job with a school district, a job with benefits. She was also going to school. I quit my job and went back to school. I was about 21. I wanted an education. I got a job working part-time in a school as a teacher's assistant."

Javier is a soft-spoken man, but I could see him reminiscing about his younger days and the drive he had to succeed. "I had met my wife's sister's boyfriend. He was a police officer for the school district. He used to come by in his uniform while I was at work to say hello. I thought it was pretty cool. I started taking classes in Administration of Justice. One day he told me Los Angeles County Sheriffs was hiring. He encouraged me to take the test. I didn't grow up wanting to be a cop, but when he told me to take the test, I talked it over with my wife. I decided to take the test. I wasn't expecting to pass. I had heard it was a really tough test. I thought, 'I'll take the test to feel it out. I'll know what to expect, and I'll make it. That way when I'm serious I'll pass.' I was now 23. I took the test, and they were calling people left and right. They didn't call my name. All these people were going up as their names were called. I was sitting there thinking they were eventually going to call everyone who was left sitting and last, and tell us we didn't pass. It turned out being the opposite; all of us who were left sitting had passed. That same day, I wasn't even prepared or anything because I had arrived to practice taking the test thinking I would fail, and they immediately sent me to my oral interview. I passed the oral, and they started scheduling me for the medical and all these other tests. I was like, 'What's going on?' I kept telling my wife, 'I got this test coming up,' and then another test would come up and I kept passing them. I passed all my tests and then all of a sudden, my testing stopped. I thought I wasn't going to make it. I had gotten to backgrounds. I didn't think a lot about it. I was still going to school and working. I didn't think I was going to make it. I then applied with the Los Angeles Police Department. I was working out, getting in shape. About a year later my background investigator from the Sheriff's Department called me. He met me and started my background investigation. One day I got a call from the Sheriff's Department. They asked me if I was ready to start. I went through class 259 in 1989 (The Sheriff's Academy classes are sequentially numbered, so this was the 259th academy class since they started numbering them). Angel was in my class.

"Angel and I didn't have many interactions with each other throughout the class. Our last names put us in different platoons. I wanted to go to a fast station. I listed East Los Angeles and Century Stations as my first choices. I got assigned to Century in 1994. It was a serious environment. The guys all had the attitude, 'Do you know what you're getting yourself into?' There was a lot of tradition from the Firestone and Lynwood Stations (Century Station was formed in 1994 and incorporated both of these former Sheriff's stations), and you were expected to perform. I knew Century was one of the fastest stations and to go there, you were going to experience the mean streets. It was not uncommon to see a murder once a week."

*****

I met Angel at a restaurant. He was having a Margarita. Man, I wanted one too. But I also wanted to keep a clear head. He is gregarious, unlike Javier who is more quiet and subdued.

I made a mistake as soon as I opened my mouth. "So, you were born in Los Angeles and grew up in Baldwin Park?"

Angel looked at me as if to say, 'Shut up.' I did, and he said, "I was born in Tijuana, Mexico, brother. I came to the United States when I was about three months old. I lived in East Los Angeles until I was about eight or nine. We then moved to Baldwin Park where I grew up. We were poor. I came from what people would consider a dysfunctional family. But I decided I was not going to be like that. I always worked. I had a friend who had a bicycle and a lawnmower. I would borrow them on the weekends. I would tie them all together on the bike and go and knock on people's doors. I would mow their grass. I would sometimes make fifty dollars on the weekend. Eventually, I got my own bicycle and lawn mower and started my own business. I gave my money to my mom to help pay the bills. I grew up boxing. I got noticed and was invited to train at a gym. I again got noticed and was asked if I wanted to fight. I was about fourteen when I got into the ring for the first time. It was funny because the guy I was going to fight was two years older than me and he was undefeated. During the fight, I just kept hitting him and moving. Hitting and moving. Although I was hitting him, I couldn't knock him out or knock him down. But he couldn't hit me; I was too fast. I think I was so fast that day because I was afraid of him. I ended up winning."

Angel was laughing and was on a roll. "I was always looking to work. I always worked hard and was never involved in anything illegal. Anyway, there was a liquor store named Rudy's Country Liquor, owned by an Asian guy named Don. Everyone in the neighborhood called it Don's liquor. So, I went into the liquor store and asked Don for a job. He asked me if I was a cholo (a gang member). I wasn't. I was a hardworking kid who had never been in trouble. The thing was I had two black eyes from fighting the boxer in the ring the day before. Don told me I looked like a cholo because I had two black eyes and probably got involved in gang fights. After I explained how I got the black eyes, Don hired me. I was a hustler, hardworking. I remember finding a case of beer in the storeroom in the back. The beer had probably been there for years. I told Don he should put the beer in the front and offer it for sale. He did, and it sold right away. We then started putting specials out, things we wanted to get rid of 'on sale.' We were selling all kinds of merchandise and people were coming in to see what the sale was going to be. Before you knew it, Don relied on me to make decisions. He knew I was straight and he trusted me. He would even go on vacations and let me run the store."

"What made you become a cop?" I was beginning to see Angel had a story for everything and this explanation was no different.

"When I was fifteen I wanted a car. I found a classic 1972 Chevrolet Monte Carlo in a junkyard. I asked the guy how much he wanted for it."

"Two hundred and fifty bucks.

"All right two hundred and fifty bucks. I bought it. The thing was it had no engine, and the windows were down. I had no way to roll the windows up because they were power windows. I met a guy at the liquor store who liked cars. I told him about my car, and he wanted to see it. He was a mechanic. When I told him about it, he asked me if it had tires.

"'No, it needs tires.' I had told him.

"'Okay I know someone who makes some nice tires. I'll get you some tires,' he said.

"I got some tires, the little low rider ones. They looked like the tires gang members used on their cars. I put them on. One hundred and fifty bucks. So, I had a car, with tires, no engine and it sat in my carport in my driveway with the windows rolled down. Everyone who I knew and who walked by said, 'Hey man, I like your ride, I like your ride.' But it had no engine. So, my buddy says, 'I can get you an engine. It's used, and I can put it in for six hundred bucks.'

"I told him, 'Yeah, but can I pay you in installments?'

"'Yeah,' he said, 'no problem.'

"I gave him two hundred fifty bucks, and I paid him in installments for his work. I never missed a payment. He put the engine in, and when I got the car back, I was all happy because the windows worked. I had the tilt steering wheel, I put on the nice mufflers, the glass paks (a type of muffler which is quite loud). I was styling. Then I drove it to Tijuana to get the upholstery done. They did my upholstery for one hundred and fifty bucks."

"How old were you?"

"Dude, I was fifteen. I didn't have a license yet. Yeah, I drove to Tijuana, no license."

We were both laughing so hard we were coughing. Then he looked at me, "Why am I talking about a car?" He was so lost in the story he had forgotten why he was telling me.

I looked at him. For the life of me, I couldn't remember either. "Oh, I wanted to know why you became a cop."

"Oh, yeah." He remembered why he was telling me this story. "I used to get pulled over all the time by the cops when I had the stupid low rider tires. Not only did I get pulled over, I got slammed on the hood, kicked in the ass, pulled by my nuts. Sheriffs, L.A.P.D., Baldwin Park P.D., they all pulled me over. I only drove on those low rider tires for two weeks, but I got pulled over all the time, every day. One time my friends and I went up Azusa Canyon to go shooting. One of my friends had a 22 rifle, and the Sheriffs pulled us over. Fuck we had a gun in the car. We were just going to have some fun shooting in the mountains. Oh, this Sheriff was a mean looking dude, and tough looking too. I was in the back seat of my car. I had a beanie on because it was cold.

"He walked up, 'Are you guys fucking gang members?'

"There were five of us, and he was alone. 'Get out of the car, you got any guns?'

"Yeah, we kind of have a 22."

"Whose gun is it?"

"I don't know, it's our friend's, but he isn't here." He was dogging us badly, but he let us go. I thought, "Shit man that's a good job."

"You liked that?"

"Yeah, I liked that."

"Why?"

"Because he had power man. Real power. But you know what, I hated him. He was a dick, but I was like, 'Wow, look how much power this guy has.' And we were all scared. Think about it. We could have whipped his ass. There were five of us, but we were scared of this guy. And he was mean, he had to be mean, he was alone. He controlled us. He was brave because he thought we were five cholos, gang members, and he wasn't afraid of us.

"So, I knew I had to change the tires on my car. I got some Uniroyals and I hardly ever got pulled over after that. But these cops had power. However, there was something I knew they didn't know. I knew what was happening on the streets. If they had treated me differently, I would have told them what was going on. I thought if I was a cop, I would be different than these guys. I would relate to people. I viewed them as not being street smart. They were just knuckle-dragging guys who pushed you around. So, I thought, 'If they could be a cop, I could be a cop.' I'm a different cop than those guys were. I don't resent them. They were doing their job to the best of their ability. But I'm a different cop than they were. I am firm, but I don't talk down to people. I don't degrade them. And I know what I'm looking for. Before I go on duty, I read all the crimes that happened the day before. I look for those cars and I look for people who meet the descriptions of those who committed the crimes. I'm not pulling over old grandmas, I'm stopping people who are potential criminals, and I am very cautious. I am not driving around in Beverly Hills. It's harder over there."

I understood what Angel was talking about. But you non-cops might not. Usually, when cops say this, it is because political correctness is expected of the officers in areas like Beverly Hills. Some cops who work in rough gang infested, dope ridden areas with high rates of violence have a hard time making the adjustment, i.e., when I transferred to West Hollywood from Lennox, I got pulled into the lieutenant's office. A sergeant and a lieutenant were there. "Robert, we've heard great things about you."

I replied, "Thank you."

The lieutenant said, "This is different than Lennox."

I replied, "Yessir."

The lieutenant said, "You have to treat people here a little different than at Lennox.

"I replied, "Yessir."

Finally, he drove the point home, "YOU CAN'T BEAT PEOPLE HERE LIKE YOU DID AT LENNOX."

I replied, "Yessir." I was dismissed.

A few hours later, I was driving around with my partner when I saw a man standing outside of the driver's door of a Cadillac. He was leaning slightly into the open window talking to another man who was the driver of the car. The guy looked my way with that deer in the headlights look. He abruptly stood up and walked away from the car. The car quickly drove away. I thought, 'I know what that is, it's a drug deal. I'd seen a bunch of them. He's selling drugs.' Now I know drug dealers are dangerous. They often have guns. So, I did the logical thing. I drove my radio car over the curb onto the sidewalk at him. Right at him. This prevents him from running or going for his gun. People panic when a car is racing at them. He was doing his job, which was thinking about which way to jump. By the time he was trying to figure it out, I had slammed on the brakes, jumped out of my car and had him on the hood of the radio car and was looking for the drugs. I searched his pockets. I looked in his shoes. I checked in the nearby drainpipes and under rocks. No luck. I figured I must've missed it. I identified him and let him go. To me, it was just another one I missed.

My partner was watching all this. After I let the guy go, he looked at me, "What the hell was that?"

I answered, "Dave, it was a dope deal."

He looked at me, "Robert, that was a male prostitute, we don't drive on sidewalks around here."

OOPS! It's different in Beverly Hills too.

Angel continued on, "I'm driving around in high crime areas. There's this apartment complex, and I've made over one hundred arrests there in the last year. If there is a problem, who do you think the manager calls? Don't you think the apartment manager loved me after that, after making all those arrests? She would call me every day. And if I was looking for someone, a lot of times she could tell me where they were. These people know me. They know who I am and that I care. I teach my trainees. I want them to learn. I ask them, 'What do you think?'

"My trainees tell me, 'I think that was amazing, sir. You had your gun pointed at him. You arrested him. You got him in the back seat. You started talking to him, and the next thing I knew he was confessing everything to you. You took him to jail, and he was thanking you.'"

"Angel, are you still a cop because you like the power of being a cop?"

"No. It's because it's the right thing to do. Look. When I was growing up, I was the victim of no less than ten or fifteen burglaries at my home. My sister was a drug user, a hype. (This is a short term for someone who uses drugs intravenously, a hypodermic syringe). All her friends used to break into my house and steal my stuff. I know how it feels to be a victim. If I can arrest a drug user, I'm stopping crime from happening. And I do it so other people don't become victims. That's why I do it. I love helping people. I love being a cop."

He looked at me, "My sister turned her life around. She's now married and a Born-Again Christian. She and her husband run a successful ministry, helping other people."

*****

The birds were singing as Javier was talking about Century station.

"The second day on patrol I handled my first shooting. The guy was lying there, and there was blood all over the place. I was green. I'd never seen anything like this before. It's so different in real life. My training officer told me to snap out of it. We still had to clear the location and make sure there were no suspects around. You had to learn fast because those streets are unforgiving. You're in survival mode all the time.

"After I got off training, I went to the C.O.P.S. team (Community Oriented Policing Services). I partnered up with Angel. We did all kinds of things. We had meetings with different community groups. But we also took a lot of people to jail. Angel came to patrol several months before me. We worked together for about a year and developed a friendship that will last forever. I haven't talked to him in a while, but I know when I do it will be just like we were together yesterday. I love him like a brother.

"Because we didn't get any calls, we could go anywhere we wanted. We got to know people in the community. We got to know who the criminals were. We were identifying gang members. We got to know the drug dealers and users. We were taking people to jail left and right. Sometimes we would stay after our shift was over, driving around looking for someone to take to jail. We were working out every day. We were in phenomenal shape. We were having a blast. Angel taught me how to box, and we sparred all the time. While we worked together, we planned things out. What if this happens or what if that happens. We knew what to do without thinking about it. We would literally drive down the street, and one of us would say, 'Draw your gun.' We would both draw our gun. We learned how to do it as the driver and the passenger without any hang-ups. We began to think alike. We had a friendship that can't be described unless you have a partner who is a cop.

"One day we stopped at the 'Indio Masonico.' It was a place where they read your cards and foretold your future. We stopped by in uniform. 'Hey, how are things around here,' just a nonchalant visit is all it was. I asked him what he did, and he said he read cards. I asked him to do a reading for me. He threw the cards and the 'Rey de Spadas,' the King of Spades, came up. He gave me a surprised look.

"I asked him, 'What does it say?'"

"He answered, 'Oh no, no. It's nothing. These are just for fun. Don't worry about it. They're just for fun.'"

"I pressed him, 'What does it say?'"

"He didn't want to tell me, but after I wouldn't let it go, he told me the cards said I would be in a big battle. I told him to do it again. He shuffled the cards and when he threw the card out the king of spades came out again. He said, 'It's nothing. Don't worry about it. These are just for fun.'"

*****

I looked at Angel. "Puppet and I are different," he said.

"Angel, who is Puppet?"

"If you see the movie *American Me*, there is a part where a prisoner is strangled by his brother. As he was choking him, he was saying, 'I'm sorry Puppet, I love you.' The guy who is getting strangled looks exactly like Javier. So, the name Puppet stuck (I looked it up. The actor is named Danny De La Paz and does look like Javier).

"Puppet is humble with a quiet personality. We always got ourselves a soda before shift. So, we had our two sodas in cups sitting inside a metal tray. One time we got a call of a rescue, and we were responding code 3 (driving with red lights and siren). Puppet was driving and grabs his soda and throws it out of the window. Then he grabs mine and throws it out of the window. (Sorry to offend you citizens, but this was a fairly common practice. If you didn't throw your soda out of the window, it usually spilled when driving on hot calls. Usually, it spilled all over you and your partner). I looked at Puppet, 'Why the fuck did you throw out my soda?' Of course, right after we lost our sodas they canceled the call. Now we were out two sodas and had to go get two more. 'Hey fucker, don't throw my soda out of the car anymore.'

"He was quiet. He couldn't believe I was cursing at him. He was the type to keep things to himself. I told him, 'We're partners. We're going to have fights. You need to let off some steam.' A couple of days later, déjà vu, we get a code 3 call. He throws his Coke out of the window. He grabs mine, and I grab it also. 'Hey let go of my Coke.' I told him. We were fighting over it. I let go with my right hand. I told him 'Let go of my Coke, I'm going to punch you if you don't let go of my soda.' He let go of my Coke. A few hours later there was a little break in the radio calls. I explained to him, 'Look we need to stay calm. Don't get excited. We can get through anything if we stay calm together.'

One day he had had enough. This was around our first week together. 'Hey motherfucker, fuck you,' he told me. 'Let's go, right here right now.' He was challenging me to fight.

I held open my arms to him. 'Finally!! Give me a hug. I love you; give me a kiss. We're married dude. We're going to have fights, but we're married. We're going to stay together. No divorce!' I meant it. We were good after that. I love him and always will.

"We practiced in the radio car. Man with a gun, draw. He was having trouble drawing his gun when he was the passenger, he would get jammed on the door. I'd look at him. 'Stupid, shift your weight, lift your ass, clear the door, draw your gun.' Then when I'd get jammed on the door, he would do it to me. 'Hey stupid, shift your weight, lift your ass, clear the door, draw your gun.' We would dog each other.

"We studied shootings. There was a shooting where the deputies shot through the windshield at two guys charging them with guns. The bullets hit the windshield and lost ninety percent of their velocity. We could see where the bullets went through the windshield and had dropped skipping off of the hood. We decided right then if we had to shoot, we would shoot outside of the car. The hard part was driving and leaning out of the driver's window. But we practiced because we knew we were going to get in a shooting. We were arresting too many hardcore gang members and criminals. It was just a matter of time. We kept practicing. I had already been in two shootings. And we were getting close. There were times where we could have shot someone but didn't. I'd look at him, or he would look at me, 'Dude we could have shot this guy, why didn't you?' It just wasn't the right time. Sometimes the gun would be right there, but we didn't see it. It's because we were trained to look at the hands. If the gun wasn't in his hand, we didn't shoot. We weren't concerned with missing a gun on a table or on a lap, we were looking at the guy's hands. If his hands were empty, we were safe.

*****

"Angel and I started our shift like every other shift, but it was not going to end like any other we had. It was October 27, 1998; it was around 10:30 a.m. I was driving, Angel was Bookman. (The Bookman is the non-driver or passenger in a radio car. He handles the radio, shotgun and so on). We were driving westbound on Florence Ave. approaching Compton Ave. Florence is a four-lane street with left turn lanes interspersed at the major intersections. The public works department was doing some roadwork, and they had the right lane blocked off with cones. As we got close to the cone pattern, a Grand Marquis cuts into our lane in front of us. I had to brake hard and slightly swerve left to avoid hitting him. I said. 'What the heck is wrong with these guys?' There were three guys in the car. We ran the car, and no wants came back. We decided to stop them and see what their hurry was."

*****

"When the car cut us off Puppet was angry. 'What's wrong with these guys? Who do they think they are?' he was saying. I wondered what kind of guys would purposely cut off a couple of cops? I was on edge.

"Puppet, calm down something's wrong. Let's use our heads. Look there's a chippie over there. When we stop them at least we'll have a little backup. Puppet turned on the lights."

*****

"Instead of pulling to the right when I turned on the lights the car kept going westbound on Florence. They then got in the left turn lane to go south on Parmalee Ave. I didn't like the fact he wanted to go to a side street, to get off a busy street. I remember looking at this Paisa (a slang term for someone from another country who doesn't know the customs of the United States). What's wrong with this guy? The driver had these glasses pulled down below his eyes and was looking at me from his driver's side mirror. I knew they knew we were behind them and were trying to stop them. "Angel, I'm going to pull alongside these guys to see who they are and to direct them to the right.'

"Angel answered, 'No don't do that. Something's wrong. Don't pull alongside them.' Angel and I listened to each other, and I decided not to pull alongside him. He makes a left onto Parmalee and doesn't stop. He doesn't run, but he doesn't stop. He keeps looking at me from his side mirror. We were making eye contact, but he didn't stop. The rear and front passenger kept looking back at us over and over again. He finally stops south of 73rd at Parmalee, but he doesn't pull all the way over to the right. He stops about a foot from the curb. I opened my door, and Angel got out. He was screaming orders at them. Just as soon as Angel got out and started yelling at them, they sped away. We chased after them. He got to 75th Street, and as he made a right, west on 75th Street, there was water in the intersection, and he fishtailed. We were right on him, and that's when things started to slow down. Through the suspect's rear tinted window, I could see the rear passenger's silhouette coming up with a rifle, an AK-47. He was sitting on the right rear side of the car. As he brought the rifle up, I could see the silhouette of the banana clip.

"I yelled out, 'AK-47, AK-47.' Time is completely slowed now. Slow motion. He leans back against the rear of the front seat, to give himself room to point the weapon at us. We're still following this guy. I can't believe it. Is this a dream? Is this real? I can't believe it is really happening. He was bringing up the rifle to his left. That's when their rear window explodes. Literally, explodes. I pulled out my gun and switched it to my left hand. I moved so slowly, but in reality, it must have been swift.

I was leaning out of the left window, the driver's window and I was firing at the car as I was driving. I looked to my right, as I was driving and firing and there was Angel. He was leaning out of the passenger's window firing at the car also. Things had slowed down so much it seemed like my gun was not working. I couldn't hear the sound of my gun going off. All I could feel was the rounds impacting our windshield, it sounded like explosions. I again slowly looked at Angel. It seemed like hours had passed. I could see the interior of the car filling with the glass of the windshield. It looked like fine dust, like smoke, like grey powdery smoke. I could feel wind passing me. It was the bullets passing me. It happened numerous times. But all super slow. It was like I was in a dream. I remember thinking something very stupid. In the academy, they told us it was against policy to shoot at fleeing vehicles. Then I thought, 'Why am I thinking this?' Then I thought, 'Why are they shooting at me? I haven't done anything to this person. Why? I haven't done any wrong to this person. Why is he trying to shoot me? This is not real.'

All the while I'm shooting, and driving, the wind is passing my head, like a muffled whooshing sound, the sound of the windshield is exploding. Angel is firing, and the car is filling up with smoke. This is not happening. I was thinking all these crazy things. What did I do to these people? I could see the windshield opening up and explode where the bullets were entering. I could hear the metallic sound of the AK-47 firing, a loud cracking metallic sound. I remember Angel trying to broadcast we were involved in a shooting. However, someone from another station was broadcasting some bullshit thing about containment or something. Angel put out a 998 (officer involved in a shooting), 75th and Hooper, 75th and Hooper. It was surreal, and I was thinking, 'How am I going to get this guy to stop shooting at us?'"

*****

"Right before Puppet lit them up (activated his lights to pull them over) he wanted to pull alongside them. 'Puppet, don't pull alongside them they're baiting us Bro. They're baiting us. Stay with me Puppet we're going to get in a shooting, they're baiting us. Stay with me!!! Bro, I need you, stay with me!!! Calm down, pay attention!!!'

"Luckily Puppet listened to me. We lit them up, and they turned left onto Parmalee. I see they're nervous. We were behind them, and they kept turning and looking at us. After about 50 yards the car slows down and starts driving on the side of the street by the curb. Wouldn't you know it, but a car from Pico Rivera (another Sheriff's Station) gets on the mic (microphone). He's swallowing the mic (talking excessively and not allowing anyone else to speak). 'Dude they're not pulling over.' They were driving so slow that I told Puppet to get right on their back, 'I'm going to get out and tell them to stop. Get ready Bro, we're going to get in a shooting, we're going to get in a shooting. Get ready.' I was thinking how screwed we were because of the Pico Rivera guy no one was going to hear us. I jumped out of the car. 'Cabrones, Motherfuckers, hands up, manos arriba! Stop your car!' They took off. When they got to 75th Street, they turned west, a right turn. They started fishtailing. That's when I hear a PPPOOOOWWWW!!! Simultaneously time slowed down. I saw in slow motion, and I could see glass flying as their rear window exploded. At the same time, I could see a hole open up in our windshield, and I could feel and hear their bullet passing through our radio car. At the same time, I knew I had to close my eyes to keep the glass from flying inside them. It all happened at the same time but not at the same time, and it all happened slowly. I was fucking like… SHIT!!! While all this was happening, Puppet was screaming 'AK-47… AK-47… AK-47.'

I was thinking 'no shit.'

We were chasing them, they were fishtailing, Puppet was out of the driver's window firing, and he was violently zig-zagging while driving.

"Goddammit Puppet, keep the car straight keep the car straight.' The way he was driving almost threw me out of the window, and I nearly lost my gun.

"Things were back to normal speed, normal time now. The suspect was

firing so fast it was amazing, BOOMBOOMBOOMBOOMBOOM-
BOOMBOOMBOOMBOOMBOOM. It was super fast. I'm firing;
boom boom boom boom boom boom boom boom. Then time slowed
down again. I'm out of bullets. I'd gone through sixteen rounds. Oh
shit. I reloaded, but as I did, I looked to my left. Things were moving so slowly, Warggggggggggggg as I reloaded. I saw Puppet leaning
out his window, and he was firing slowly. Oh shit, this shit is real,
Waaaaaarrrggggh.

"I was thinking I was going to die. I was thinking Puppet was going to
die. I was scared and sad. It was going to happen, I was going to die. I
knew it. Then I saw my wife and my kids. My kids were just looking
at me: my son, my daughters, I could see their faces. But my wife had
her hands over her face, and she was crying. I couldn't understand why
I was seeing this. I couldn't believe it. That enraged me. Something
else got into me. To think these guys were going to take me away from
my wife and kids infuriated me. 'Fuck these guys, they're not going
to kill me.' It was all taking forever. The shooting, me shooting, Puppet shooting, the suspects shooting, the car exploding, glass flying, my
family's faces, it was forever.

"They tried to turn left on Hooper, but they were going too fast and
crashed into some parked cars parked on the west side of the Hooper
and 75th Street. We were right on their ass. I could see the shooter
was trying to get his rifle up on us again. He was all messed up from
the crash but was trying to get his bearings. I was out of the car again.
I was shooting and had run out of ammo for the second time. I had
now gone through thirty-one rounds. I had one magazine left. Fifteen
bullets.

"Now things were speeding up again. I could see the driver's door open.
I yelled at Puppet, 'Get the guy with the AK, get the guy with the AK.
As we were firing into the back window, I could see the AK guy jerk-
ing all over the place as we were hitting him. Puppet and I were both
hitting him. 'Puppet, back up, BACK UP, REVERSE WE'RE TOO
CLOSE, BACK THE FUCK UP!' Puppet backed up the car about

sixty feet. As we were backing up, I was firing. When we stopped, I got out and went to the rear of the radio car."

*****

"When the car got to Hooper it crashed into some parked cars. Then it got weird. It seemed like it disappeared for a second. I don't know why. But I learned a car going north on Hooper clipped the rear of the suspect's vehicle, which made it crash it into some parked cars on Hooper. Even though this event should have been in my vision because it was right in front of me, I never saw it. When the car crashed it knocked the guy with the AK around so he couldn't fire at us. Everything was moving in frames, like plop… plop… plop… plop. It was not a continuous visual picture, it was like in frames. Frame frame frame frame, and it was all extremely slow. When he crashed my instinct was to ram their car. I wanted to ram them into a solid wall. Angel was yelling at me, 'Stop, stop, stop. You're getting too close.' He was right. So, I put it in reverse and backed up.

"The guy in the back seat was now up again and firing his AK at us. The driver was bailing out of the driver's door, and he was firing at us with a handgun. The passenger had bailed out of the passenger door and had run across the front of their car. He was also firing at us. He and the driver had taken cover behind the car parked on Hooper they had crashed into. I was completely focused on the guy with the AK-47. I was still sitting in the car, and I was in disbelief. I wanted to get out of the car. A round came through the windshield and pierced the steering wheel. I can't tell you why I did this, but at the same instant the bullet came through, I opened the car door and rolled to my left. I was still sitting inside the car but was hanging out between the interior of the car and the wedge of the door where it met the car. I remember the round coming through. I felt the force and full impact of the round. I remember feeling it really close to me, and I remember it burning. Then I was pushed back into my seat.

"I was in hell. I blacked out. I don't know how long I was out, but it must not have been that long. I honestly thought I had been killed. At the time I blacked out, I couldn't hear anything anymore. I couldn't see anything anymore. Everything was dark. It seemed like an eternity. I completely lost track of time. I didn't know where I was hit. I thought I was dead. I remember opening my eyes and hearing things again. I realized I was still in hell. I looked to my right, and Angel was no longer there, but his door was wide open. I remember Angel yelling, 'GET BACK HERE, GET BACK HERE!!!' When I opened my eyes, I touched where I was burning with my left hand. Right on the right side of my right triceps. I looked at my hand, and I saw blood. I touched my face, and I saw blood. I touched my head, and I saw blood. I touched my neck, and I saw blood. I was still sitting in the car and wondering, 'Am I dead?' I remember looking at the gun in my hand and moving my hand. I saw my hand move. It was amazing to me. I thought, 'I must not be hurt that bad.' I remember self-assessing myself. I took a deep breath. I realized I could breathe. I said to myself, 'I can breathe fine, so I must be okay. I gotta be okay.' Then I wanted to get out of the car, staying in the car is a death trap. I found out later the AK guy was firing into my car door. When I opened my door and rolled to my left, he started firing into the door. He was tracking me. If I had gotten out right when I opened my door, I probably would have been killed. Those AK rounds will go right through a door. It just wasn't my time. That's the only way I can understand it. These guys were not trying to get away. It seemed like they wanted to fight. They were on a mission. Their mission was not to just shoot and scare us and get away. It seemed more personal. They wanted to kill us. There was no doubt in my mind that's what they wanted to do.

"I got out of the car and started firing in their direction. I crouched/walked to the rear of the car. While I was going to the back of the car, Angel is yelling at me, 'Get the shotgun, get the shotgun.' I remember distinctly thinking, 'Fuck no, I'm not going to get the shotgun! These guys are shooting up front.' It was too dangerous man. I didn't want to get the shotgun; I wanted to get the fuck to the back of the radio car.

"I crossed behind Angel. He was at the rear of the radio car on the driver's side. So now I was on the passenger side of the rear of the radio car. I got down on one knee. I remember looking up at Angel, and I was thinking, he's going to look down at me and tell me, 'You're fucked up. You're going to die.'"

*****

"The driver is out of the car; the front passenger is out of the car. They took cover behind the crashed car and are firing at us. Time slowed again. The guy with the AK is out of the car and is on his belly crawling on the street on the passenger side of the car. He was barely moving. The AK is lying about ten feet behind him. So, I'm at the back of the car, and I'm yelling at Puppet, 'Get the fucking shotgun! Get the fucking shotgun!' He was coming out of the radio car toward me. I was on my last magazine. My last fifteen bullets. The guys behind the car were now shooting at Puppet as he was coming to me. As Puppet was heading to me, I was laying down cover fire, keeping the suspects heads down so Puppet wouldn't get shot. Bam bam bam bam bam, rapid fire. By the time Puppet got to me I was out of bullets. Out of the corner of my eye, I look at Puppet 'Bro are you all right? You all right?'

"Yeah, I'm good. I'm good,' he's telling me. Then nothing happened for a little bit, there was a lull. Then I saw the front seat passenger suspect duck walking toward the AK that was lying in the street. I went to Puppet and pointed to the guy trying to get to the AK. He said, 'I'm out of bullets, I'm out of bullets!'

"I responded, 'So am I.' He grabbed his backup weapon, a two-inch five-shot handgun. I told him, 'Save it in case they charge us.' I told him, 'Stay here.' And I looked at him, and his face was gray. I knew something was wrong. I wanted to check him out, but I was worried the front passenger would get to the AK. If that happened, I knew we would be killed. I stood up and screamed, 'AHHHHH MOTHER-FUCKER!!!' I was running and screaming and pointing my empty Beretta at the front passenger. I could see his face. He was scared out of his mind. He dove back behind the crashed car. Time was really slow. Each step was like a mile. 'AHHHHHH!!!' I yelled as I ran. I could see the driver so slowly shooting at me. Now I was pointing my empty gun at him as I ran through his gunfire. I got to the driver's door of the radio car and got to the shotgun. I stepped out of the car and started firing the shotgun. Boom, Boom, Boom, Boom. The windows are smashing, I was blowing up the car they were hiding behind. It wasn't until this point, 56 seconds after the shooting started, that dispatch was able to clear the air and heard our broadcast that we were involved in a shooting. 56 seconds. To me it was 56 years. No one heard us because the deputy at Pico Station was eating the mic.

"Another deputy was on Parmalee and thought he heard fireworks. He said to himself, 'Who is firing off fireworks in October?' Then he heard us on the radio and realized he was right around the corner. He came and started shooting alongside me at the suspects.

"All of a sudden I hear Puppet screaming at the back of the radio car. 'I'M HIT! I'M HIT!' I looked back and he's standing up. His face is gray, he was staggering around, and blood was shooting out of his neck. He's obviously in shock and is walking like a zombie. His blood is spurting out with every beat of his heart and shooting out about five feet. I yelled, 'GET DOWN, GET DOWN!!!' I could see the blood landing on the trunk of our radio car."

Angel's eyes welled up as he told me this and his voice got low.

"I uh, I uh… I thought he was going to die. My partner was going to die, and I couldn't help him. That's what I was thinking. I still had two suspects. The AK suspect had stopped moving and was lying in the street. But there were still two left."

*****

"When I was on my knee at the back of the radio car Angel was looking at me, 'C'mon, c'mon.' It never dawned on me Angel was looking at my left side. My injuries were pretty much on my right side. Angel was firing at the suspects, first firing to the left then to the right. Time was still very slow for me. I was still thinking I was going to die. Then I thought, 'You know what? Fuck these motherfuckers!' I said to myself, 'I'm okay. I'm not going to die. I'm going to be fine because Angel isn't saying shit to me. He's not saying I'm hurt. So, I must be okay. I must not be hurt that bad. I can move my hand, I can breathe fine, I'm not going to sit here and die. I'm going to fire back.' I peeked out of the right side of the radio car, and that's when I saw the AK suspect low-crawling on the street. He was crawling away from the back of the car toward the parked cars. I thought, 'I do not want that man getting his hands on that AK again, and I'm going to shoot him as many times as I can.' I started skipping rounds at him (deliberately shooting into the ground in front of a suspect and in effect ricocheting rounds into him). The next thing you know my gun was empty. I reloaded. Again, I started skipping rounds. The suspect was still crawling. I realized, 'I've got to stop this guy.' I slowly and deliberately looked through my sights and started taking careful aim at the suspect. I started hitting him. I could see the cloth of his clothes going into his body as the bullets struck him. I was wondering, 'Why isn't he stopping? I can see my bullets hitting him, but he's not dying. Why doesn't he stop moving? He's still moving.' I was putting a lot of bullets into him. All of a sudden, he stopped moving. I knew he was no longer a threat, so I stopped shooting him.

"The two other suspects were shooting one shot at a time. One would shoot then duck behind the car. Then the other would shoot then duck. I started firing at them. I remember hearing a canon to my right. It was Angel shooting the shotgun. I never knew he ran back to the radio car and got the shotgun and was firing it. I then saw one of the windows of the car the suspects were hiding behind disintegrate. Next, I saw the suspects go down. I thought, 'He fucking hit 'em!' It wasn't so because as soon as he stopped shooting, both of them got up and began shooting again.

"Again, my gun was empty. I got another magazine out and went to put it in my gun, and it was my pepper spray, not another magazine. I was out of ammunition. I thought I had gone through two magazines when I had actually gone through three. 46 bullets. I was thinking, "We're fucked. These guys are not going to go away. These guys are not here to scare us off.' They were there to kill us. I was afraid. I mean I was afraid throughout the whole ordeal, but there were times when the anger overtook the fear. I was thinking, 'I've got five shots left. If these motherfuckers want to charge at us, it's going to be hand to hand.'

"I saw a radio car speeding north on Hooper. I screamed in my radio, 'STOP, STOP, STOP. He went right through the kill zone, right through the firefight. I thought, 'What's wrong with this stupid ass? He's going to get killed.' As it passed the suspects, I saw it was a CHP officer. They had been dispatched to the scene because of a crash.

"I don't know if I was going into shock. All of a sudden one our partners was there. He looked at me. He said, 'Oh fuck, I've got to get you to a doctor.' He scared me. I was wondering, 'Do I look fucked up or what?' I heard Angel asking for rescue to respond. Everybody started showing up. I had this thing going through my mind, 'Don't tell me I'm fucked up, okay? Don't tell me I'm hurt. Don't tell me I'm going to die. I don't need to hear that.' The deputies got there, and they started looking at me with wide eyes, 'OH MY GOD, OH MY GOD! Hey, let's throw him in the car, throw him in the patrol car.' The next thing I knew I was being ushered into the backseat of a patrol car. A deputy was riding with me in the back seat of the radio car. I had a death grip on the mic. He had to pry my hand off of it. The next thing I knew I was at the door of Saint Francis Medical Center and the next thing I knew I was naked. They were looking over every inch of my body. They gave me something, and I was happy."

*****

Angel was describing the crime scene: "A lot of deputies started showing up. The two suspects just gave up. The AK-47 suspect was dead. I looked around, and Puppet was gone. I was pissed. That is a gross understatement. I wanted to kill these guys, and they had just given up. I was crying. They had killed my partner. I was out of control and beyond enraged and beyond grief. At that moment, nothing mattered to me. Nothing. I went to the driver, 'You killed my partner you fucking COBARDE (COWARD).' I wanted him to know. He could see in my eyes my intent to kill him. I wanted to kill him. I was crying. A deputy named Danny and Deputy Jerry Ortiz were there.

"I reached into my pocket where my backup gun was located.

"Jerry quickly slapped my hand away from my pocket and took my gun from my pocket. 'It's not worth it man.'

"Jerry, if you love me… if you're my brother, you'll give me my gun. This motherfucker shouldn't be alive. He doesn't deserve it.'

"Homes, I'm your brother that's why I'm doing this." Jerry saved my life.

"Sergeant Beauchamp Hyde showed up. What a great guy. He asked me, 'What happened Angel?'

"I want to go see my partner. If you'll take the handle. (To take the handle means to take over control of the incident. In the Sheriff's Department, the deputy who receives the call is in control of the call unless a superior officer officially tells the subordinate he will take control. It doesn't matter if the Sheriff himself shows up, the deputy is in control of the situation until properly relieved. That's why Los Angeles County Deputies are trained to think and are expected to make decisions). I'll tell you what happened. I want to go see my partner. He's been shot. He's going to die.'"

"What happened?"

Angel's voice was now a whisper as he recounted the incident, "You're standing on his blood, Sarge." The Sergeant looked around. I pointed and asked him, 'Do you see the trunk? Look at the trunk Sarge, that's his blood.' Beauchamp's eyes got watery."

As this unbelievably tough cop who was sitting in front of me told me this, his eyes misted over, mine did too.

"'Angel tell me what happened really quick,' he asked me.

"So, I told him.

"'Go on now go.' He told me.

"One of the deputies took me to the hospital. I was praying, 'Please God, save him. I don't want him to die.' A lot of brass (Department Executives) were at the hospital. They were lined up trying to shake my hand as I walked by them. I ignored them all. I walked in Puppet's room, and there he was sitting in his underwear. He had an I.V. in his arm, a patch on his arm and a patch on his neck. 'I thought you were dead.' I went over and gave him a hug and a kiss. He pushed me away.

"'Get away from me you fag.'

"He looked high. I looked at his I.V. 'What the hell is in that I.V.?'

"'I don't know, but it feels good, whatever is in there.'"

*****

Javier was looking at me, "I can't tell you why I rolled to my left when I was in that radio car. But it saved my life. I don't know when I got it, but I had a huge bruise on my right rib cage. Another bullet? I don't know. When the bullet came through the window, it hit the steering wheel. Even so, it had the force to push me back against the seat. It fragmented the steering wheel. Shrapnel went into my head and neck, just all over the right side of my neck and head. I have a little jar I collect them in. Sometimes the pieces of metal work their way out of my skin, and I put them in the jar."

*****

Angel was now laughing, "When Javier got out of the hospital my wife and I picked him up. 'Puppet, do you want to see the radio car? It's at the station at the pumps.' He said yes. The car was riddled with bullets. It was disabled. They killed it. We looked inside, and there were numerous bullet holes in both the driver's and passenger's backrests where we sat. It's a good thing we had practiced shooting while leaning out of the car.

"As we were looking at the car, and I was wondering how we survived, I looked at Puppet. 'Look, Bro.' I pointed at the seat between the passenger and driver, where our metal tray sat. And right there on top of the metal tray they sat. Our two cups of Coke. Not a drop was spilled. They were just hanging out together. His and mine. Partners. Partners who could not be separated by wild driving, flying glass or gunfire. Partners who stood by each other through thick and thin. Coke partners."

*****

You readers have seen as you read this story the sequence of events is different between the two storytellers. Maybe some things said were different or were heard differently between the two storytellers. Just to make it very clear to you, these storytellers have recounted the story as it unfolded for them. Some lawyers might try to use these seeming inconsistencies as proof they are lying. That the event did not happen as they say. I guarantee if I put two of you through the scenario, for real, with real bullets, you would not recount the incident the same. No one is lying here; to each of them, this is how it happened.

*****

There is a training class put on by the Los Angeles County Sheriff's Department named Laser Village. This training is designed to put deputies through live scenarios where tactics are taught and to help deputies understand when to shoot and when not to shoot. Angel and Javier went to this class together. During the class, one of the instructors asked if anyone there had been in a shooting. Javier and Angel told their story. Everyone in the class cried. Imagine twenty or so deputies who have seen death numerous times, in the class crying in front of everyone else.

*****

To you readers, just to help you understand the intensity and violence faced by the south-central patrol deputies let me explain. Deputy Jerry Ortiz was killed in the line of duty several years after this incident. Shot by some parolee not worth mentioning.

Danny who is mentioned in the same sentence with Deputy Jerry Ortiz at the end of this story had a trainee who was killed in 1992. His name was Deputy Nelson Yamamoto. He was gunned down, shot multiple times by an illegal alien.

The sergeant mentioned at the end of this book, Sergeant Beauchamp Hyde, died of a massive heart attack in his young forties. He was just as real a victim as any officer gunned down.

*****

Homicide surmised the suspects, in this case, were part of a cartel and were protecting a drug shipment.

*****

Angel has been a successful father, and together with his wife of 27 years, they raised a beautiful family. His two daughters are successful dance choreographers. His son played professional baseball for six years. After his baseball career ended, he has followed in his father's footsteps. He is now honorably serving the community as a Los Angeles County Deputy.

*****

Javier Valencia and Angel Jaimes received the Medal of Valor for their actions on the morning of October 27, 1998. This is the department's highest award and honor bestowed upon its members.

Chapter 11

A Cop's Cop

20th Street and Olive Ave., Long Beach, CA

When Rick first met me, he didn't like me. See, I am a jokester. Not that I play practical jokes on people. I think that is mean. But I find humor in everyday little things. Some would say I'm sarcastic.

Rick says I'm damaged.

He would know.

I used to sit in the cubicle across and one down from him. Every morning when I would get to work, I would whistle to Rick. It was my way of saying good morning to him.

Rick didn't like it. He told me, "Who do you think you're whistling to? I'm not some dog!" He would then turn away and go back to work.

I understood that. My dad doesn't like people whistling at him. Or calling him by putting up their hand, palm up and curving their index finger backward repeatedly, you know, "Come here." It's a Mexican thing. I guess they consider it disrespectful.

Now, when Rick is sitting in his cubicle, I sneak behind him, give a little whistle, and he turns around. I get a, "Oh, hi Bobby," and a smile.

When I first saw Rick, he intimidated me a bit. I don't mean his looks. I mean his attitude. Rick is loud. When he talks, you can hear him across the room. He punctuates his sentences with swear words, and slang terms. They are as much a part of him as breathing. He is bald. Now that he is older he has some fat on him, but you can see that hard, thick muscle behind it all. He looks really tough.

I love Rick. It took me a while to get to love him. Let me tell you why. It takes a while to get to know someone, and Rick, although he talks, is a bit vague about himself. If he doesn't trust you, or like you, he will be polite as hell, and he won't tell you anything.

Here is what I love about Rick. He is what most people would consider a man. A real man. Not a pretend man, like these guys you see strutting around. He is not a braggart. He is a humble person. He has no patience for those who would hurt innocents. He would do anything to help someone in need if it was in his power. He loves his family. He works hard. Even though he is damaged like me.

Piece by piece I got to know Rick. Piece by piece I grew to respect him and his values. Make no mistake, he's imperfect like we all are. He's made mistakes like we have, but he cares about doing the right thing.

*****

Ricky, as we all call him, was born in Downey, California. He grew up in Pico Rivera. In the land of the Green Meanies. Rick was the first to introduce me to the term.

"Bobby," he spoke as he yelled to me, "I love the Sheriff's Department." He smiled and gave that faraway look that is so much a trademark of his as is his bald head. "The Green Meanies! Fuck they used to kick our ass. It was known, don't fuck with the Green Meanies."

I figured it out. The Los Angeles County Sheriff's Department, of which I had been a member of, wore tan shirts and green pants. We did have a reputation of taking care of business on the streets and in the jails. Thus, Rick used the term the Green Meanies.

I smiled back at Rick. "Rick, it was the only way to win. I don't think non-criminals should fear the cops, but the criminals should be deathly afraid of us."

"Bobby, I could see all the cities, including L.A.P.D., were getting their power taken away from them by non-cop mayors and city council members. And the fucking media. How in the hell could they pass judgment on us before the facts came out? These are people who have no idea what it's like to deal with really bad criminals."

He got that faraway look again. What Rick does is tilt his head back a little. He looks out like he is on top of a mountain looking at a beautiful mountain higher up. Looking at God's own creation. When he does this, his eyes are half closed, and he looks as if he's thinking something you couldn't possibly understand. "Then you had the Sheriffs. The Sheriff is an elected official. There are no civilians telling him what to do. If the people don't like what he is doing or how he runs his department, they can vote him out. It never happens. Sheriffs are in office for twenty years. I always said if the criminals ever lose their fear of the Sheriff, we will lose control of the criminals. They are the last line."

"Rick did you ever actually see the Green Meanies in action?"

"Hell yes! Bobby, my brother, God rest his soul, had some problems."

I looked at Rick.

"Bobby, he would go on binges. I don't know what he would use, but I think he would do different stuff. Heroin, marijuana, reds, you name it. I don't know everything he used, but he really gave our family hell. He would yell at us. Mom, Dad, all of us. I loved him, but I was scared of him. He was seven years older than me. And he was big. About my height, and stocky. Really solidly built. He had huge calves. One time he came home from one of his binges. He had been gone about three days. He came home with a new white station wagon Vega. Do you remember those cars?" Rick looked at me and raised his eyebrows. That's another thing he does.

"Yeah Rick, they're kind of little shit cars."

"Exactly. Anyway, I loved my brother. When he showed up, I went inside his car and searched it. I was twelve. I was scared he would find me doing it. But he didn't. I pulled down the driver's visor, and two big baggies fell on my face. One was full of marijuana, and the other was full of reds. I took them in the house. I got two more big baggies and put oregano in one. Then I put a bunch of red one-day vitamins in the other baggie. I flushed the marijuana and the reds down the toilet. Then I went back to the car and put the baggies back in the visor."

"Why Rick? Why'd you do that?"

"I wanted to save him. I wanted him to stop terrorizing the house. He was tearing the family apart with his behavior. I thought he was going to hurt someone in the family, or someone would kill him. Even through all that, I loved him." Rick had an impassive look on his face. "Anyway, at some point he went to the car and found out his drugs were gone. He lost it. He was cussing and yelling, 'Did you take 'em Rick? You took 'em!' He started his car and drove up to the porch and tried to drive his car through the house. He was sitting in the car and revving the engine, trying to get the car to drive through the house. I was terrified. I was a little kid. My mom was on the porch. I went around to the back of the house. I went through the house to the front door to be with my mom."

"Why didn't you go up the front of the porch?"

"Because the Vega was blocking the way! My mom went in the house and said she had no choice but to call the Sheriffs. Pico Rivera Sheriff's Station. When she hung up, she was crying. She kept saying she had no choice. It hurt her to have to do it. She was really scared."

Rick and I were talking at a Denny's Restaurant as he was telling the story. As he was talking, he was gathering all the dirty dishes on the table together and piling them on top of one another. He smiled, "Bobby, my mother always told me when I was done eating, 'Gather your dirty dishes together and go wash them.'"

I smiled and laughed.

"By now the neighbors were out, trying to talk to my brother. Trying to talk him down. But he was crazy bad. The thing is when he was not on drugs, he was a nice guy. He would do anything for you. He was still yelling, 'You took 'em Rick! Did you take 'em?' I didn't know what to say, I was a little kid. The Sheriffs showed up. They yanked him out of the car and took him to jail."

The waitress came by. Rick looked at her as she took the plates he had piled up. Then in a rather loud voice, he said, "Thank you ma'am."

"Would you like some more coffee?"

"Oh yes ma'am. Thank you ma'am. That'd be very nice ma'am."

After she poured us another cup, Rick again looked at her, "Thank you ma'am. Appreciate it ma'am!"

He looked at me and lowered his voice, "Where was I sir?"

"We were talking about your brother."

"Oh, yes sir, Bobby. Sir, let me tell you another time. I can't remember why the deputies came to our house. It was about my brother. When they showed up, my brother came out on the porch. The deputies were on our front lawn. The deputies were talking to my brother, 'Come on down, let us help you. We just want to talk to you.' My brother was off his head again. He was cussing the deputies, the Green Meanies. I thought, 'Oh oh this is not going to be good.' He stepped off of the porch onto the lawn and put up his fists. He said, 'Let's see what you got.' One of the deputies hit him in the head with a flashlight. P'shew."

Rick made a motion with his hand standing straight up and then falling flat. "My brother went down, and the Green Meanies put the boots to him. You know Bobby, your environment doesn't have to dictate who you become. For instance, my brother was married to a wonderful woman who divorced him. She raised their son, my nephew, to be a great husband and father. I am proud to call him my nephew. He is just like my brother was when he was sober. He'll do anything for you."

"Ricky didn't that make you hate the deputies, cops? After you saw them beat your brother?"

"No Bobby! No sir," Rick talked, yelled at me as he raised his eyebrows. "I was thankful. They came to help us. They did the right thing. He was out of control."

"Ricky, I'm surprised you became a cop after that."

He became contemplative again, that faraway look. "I became a cop in 1985. I was 27. I..." Rick stalled out. He quit talking. He looked embarrassed.

"What?" I asked him.

"It sounds really corny. But I wanted to help people. I wanted to make a difference. I wanted to be like the deputies who helped our family when no one else could. I still want to help people. It never goes away. Every day. It bothers me when innocent people get hurt. It always bothered me, but it bothers me more now because I can't do anything about it. I can't understand why some cops lose that or choose not to be in a radio car."

Ricky was a street cop to the core. Where it really counted.

*****

Rick and I left the Denny's Restaurant. It was filling up. We found a park in Montebello, a city on the outskirts of Los Angeles. It was nice in the sun.

"On April 29, 2000, I had been working the Gang Enforcement Unit of the Long Beach Police Dwpartment for eight years. My partner had worked the unit two years. We had only worked together two weeks."

"Did you know him well?"

"No Bobby. No one really knew him well. He wasn't a drinker. He worked out. The one time I got him to go to the cop bar with us, he drank Near Beer (a non-alcoholic beer tasting beverage). He finally had a beer and became a little loud. It was a side none of us cops had ever seen before."

Rick got a sparkle in his eye. "I used to drive a blue plain wrap." (A plain wrap is a term to indicate an unmarked police or radio car). "I kept it clean Bobby." That faraway look again.

Now I got a sparkle in my eye. Rick's cubicle is the dirtiest, nastiest one in our unit. "Why Rick? Why did you keep your unit clean?"

"Bobby, it's where we did business. Our hands were always on the hood of our car. I would lay papers on the hood and write on it. Many times, I would eat on it. I didn't want to have a layer of dust or dirt on it. That would dirty our hands, then our uniform, and paperwork."

Rick explained his job. "Bobby, there were and are a lot of gangs in Long Beach. One gang alone had upwards of 700 members, sir. There were at least ten gangs spread out over probably five square miles. They were shooting each other. It was a race war. The Blacks and Hispanics were shooting each other. The Asians were shooting the Hispanics. They were robbing people. They were dealing drugs. We had 35 to 40 gang guys. Hard chargers. We were busy every night. We shook them up. We identified them. We took them to jail. I was straight up with them. I wasn't mean to them unless they asked for it. Only if I had to be. They dictated if I should turn it on or off."

"Rick, what day was April 29?" I knew he would know.

"Oh, it was a Saturday sir. We were working from 3 p.m. to 1 a.m. I was driving. We were in a predominately black area. The week before, one our officers shot a crip (this is a member of the crips gang) at a shithole motel at Pacific Coast Highway and Chestnut Ave. I had been there helping with the crime scene. We were very close to the area where this occurred. My partner and I did an F.I.R. (this is usually a short card filled out that identifies people and if they have any gang affiliations) on a couple of guys. One of them was on parole. Our sergeant had been there while we were filling out the F.I.R. Right after we filled out the F.I.R. I got a call from our probation officer who worked closely with us. She was available to us all the time, for people we arrested on probation, or for probation searches. Anyway, she called me and asked me to get some ice for the beer."

"What beer?"

"She had some beer in her car and wanted me to get some ice. I told her I was going to the Seven Eleven to get some ice. We were going to meet and put the beer on ice so it would be cold when we got off duty. Our unit sometimes met with her after shift, and we all cooled down. You know, decompress."

"Yep, I understand. You guys were close."

"Yeah Bobby. We were very close. Who else could understand what we saw and went through? Anyway, after the call, we left the street and were driving to Seven Eleven. It was about 10:20 p.m. I was driving westbound on 20th Street. When I got to Olive Ave., I made a left. As soon as I made the left, I saw eight to ten Hispanics gathered about 30 to 40 yards away. They were on the west side of the street. I stopped my car and parked on the west side of the street. The Hispanics looked at us with that deer in the headlights look. You know that 'Oh shit look!' I said to my partner, 'Who in the fuck are those guys?' One of the guys crossed Olive eastbound, never taking his eyes off us. He just eye fucked us as he crossed the street. I said to my partner, 'Let's get him, and let's watch those other guys.' I was referring to the eight to ten guys milling around. Like I said, I was parked on the west side of the street of the car, and it was in park. Before we could get out of the car, I heard a shot. Bobby, it was an AK-47."

"Rick, it was a crack."

"Exactly sir."

"A handgun goes pop, a rifle, an AK-47 has a loud, distinctive crack. A hard sound."

"Oh yes sir. That's it."

There was a little silence. He continued, "Three things happened at once. I heard the crack; time immediately slowed down to waaaaarrrrggg (as Rick said this he put his hands in front of him, palms together and slowly pulled them away from each other while slowly spreading his fingers); and the passenger window, which was rolled up exploded into the car. I thought, 'OH FUCK!!! WE ARE SO FUCKED!!!' That thought filled my head before the second shot came. The shots came into the car very very fast but time was slowed so much it seemed very slow. It's hard to explain. Bobby, the inside of the car was evaporating. My partner was now leaning against my right shoulder. He was motionless. He had not said a word. Then it happened; a sudden searing and piercing pain in the side of my head. It knocked the wind out of me. I couldn't breathe. It was like a huge Samoan hit me in the head with a sledgehammer. How could a hit to the head knock the breath out of me? I'd been shot in the head. It was the worst pain I'd ever had."

Rick has a divot, a little scoop on the right side of his head, with a scar covering it.

He pointed to the scar, "Bobby, on a scale of one to ten, the pain was a ten. I don't know, but I think I had a concussion. Things were fuzzy, and it hurt so bad, so very bad, I couldn't believe the body could have such pain and survive. Even though I wasn't completely there because of the force of the bullet and the pain, I was. The car, the inside of the car was evaporating, disintegrating. Metal, dust, glass, plastic. All of it was flying around inside the car, and the car, it was coming apart. I was in a daze. Things were going so slow, forever, and ever. I wanted it to end, I knew I was going to die. I lost track of time. And then I was back. My partner was leaning against me motionless. I wondered if he was dead. I thought, 'Oh my God, if we both die it is going to look so bad for the department.' What a thought huh? Weird that I would worry about the department's reputation at a time like that." Rick had that raised eyebrow look.

"Subconsciously I knew the shooter was pulling the trigger as fast as he could, but everything was in slow motion. The back of the car was getting peppered with bullets, shattering everything in its path. I didn't know it at the time, but my partner had been shot in the head also. I don't know when that happened. He hadn't made a sound. He never made a sound. Again, I thought and pleaded to no one, I guess it was to God. 'When are the shots going to stop?' It seemed like it was going on forever. Then it happened again. I got shot in the abdomen. I think it hit my vest because there was no stomach wound I know of. But when the bullet hit my stomach it buckled my whole body forward. I lurched forward from the force of the impact. It threw me forward. I couldn't move. Suddenly and instantaneously I could not move. Amidst all of the chaos I became terrified, 'Oh fuck I'm paralyzed.' I was scared. Really scared because I couldn't move. I thought, 'I'm missing a chunk of my head. Must be missing a chunk of my head because I'm paralyzed, and my head hurts so very unbelievably much.' I must have realized at that point my partner was dead because I thought, 'They're going to kill me too!' The excruciating pain mixed with paralyzing fear and my inability to move. Everything inside the car was still coming apart and flying around. Then it happened again. My right leg slammed into my left leg. Instant pain at the maximum pain the body could feel. Unbelievable excruciating pain. My hand went down to my right knee while at the same time I looked down. The bottom portion of my leg and my foot were laying at some God-awful, sickening, unnatural angle. It hurt like a motherfucker Bobby. I can't describe it. The bullet came through my knee and out of my inside upper calf muscle."

Rick was wearing shorts. I hadn't looked at his leg since that morning, but I looked now. An ugly pucker showed on the inside upper calf of his right knee.

Rick went on, "I thought, 'I've got to put out a broadcast. I got to get some help.' I noticed the shooting had stopped. I thought, 'I can't scream. I have to talk normally. Everybody has to understand me so they can find me.' I grabbed the microphone, 'Emergency traffic, emergency traffic, emergency traffic. Gang 14 my partner and I have been shot! We're at 20th and Lime!' We weren't, we were at 20th and Olive. I had put out the wrong location. I was scared. I thought, 'The shooter is reloading, he's going to kill us both.' It was a terrifying idea I might have to go through it again. You can see I had no idea how my partner was. I thought, 'I've got to get the fuck out of here. I've got to get home to my kids.' My thinking became so acute I remembered the Los Angeles County Sheriff's George Arthur shooting. In an officer survival class, I once took, I remembered him saying, 'Whatever you do, don't give up. Ever.' It was like a link clicked on in my head. His words came back to me. 'Don't you EVER give up, NEVAHH!!!' Now my wife, my kids, my mom, my dad, and my family they all came to my thoughts. 'Don't give up Rick,' they said to me. I had to get the fuck out of there before he started shooting again. Up to this point, there was no doubt in my mind I was going to die. Now that the shooting had stopped I thought I maybe had a chance. Bobby, you know, going through this yourself, this was all happening in milliseconds. I honestly can't tell you how long it had been from the first shot to this point, but it was certainly less than a minute. Probably more like 10 seconds. The dispatcher's name was Melina. The one person who was listening to me to help me. If they could have handed out an Oscar for exceptional performance, she would have won. She said to me, 'Help's coming, don't give up.' It was like the sun on a rainy day. She gave me light. She saved me. Her words. How she said it. God bless her. It's weird. I was deaf. I mean I could not hear normal sounds of the city, the traffic, or cars, but I could hear her. The rest of the world was soundless. Weird. Sometime throughout this whole thing I had scooted down as low as I could in the seat. I was huddled next to my partner. He was six feet tall and two hundred sixty pounds. All muscle. I was thinking if bullets came from his way, maybe his body would stop them from hitting me. I was really scared to have the thought and hope the bullets would hit my partner so I wouldn't get shot again. It's just terrible I had that thought, but I did."

Rick was gracious enough to let me hear the radio transmission he put out that night. I knew it was his voice, but it was someone else talking. It haunts me to this day.

After I got shot, Sean brought me a copy of my radio transmission. As it was playing, my wife rubbed the back of her arms as chills ran down them. She later told me she could tell by my voice I was worried about dying. In the transmission, I repeat over and over again in futile attempts to get help, the only street I can recall, "Norton...Norton... Norton." I am not crying, but I am obviously very, very, scared. My voice had an unearthly soft wailing, begging sound to it while in between each word you can hear me trying to catch my breath.

Rick's transmission was chillingly similar. He did the same thing as me. He repeated the street he was on, "Olive," several times but he could not come up with the cross street. His voice was plaintively quiet, softly begging and earnestly beseeching. I cried when I heard his transmission. "Help me... Help me... Olive... Olive... Olive." You then hear a transmission from a male dispatcher that numerous neighbors reported shots were being fired at Olive and 19th Street and units are responding. Rick then transmits again begging and entreating the poor dispatcher who, when she talks, is obviously desperately trying to get units to him to help him, "Help me... I love my kids... Don't let me die, Ma'am."

"Melina had broadcast my position to other units, and I hoped they were coming. I slid my left leg against my right leg, shoving my right leg out of the way. More pain, almost more than I could bear. I pressed on the gas. The engine just revved. The car was in park. I reached up and put the car in drive. I was so afraid to put my head up. But I had to drive out of there. I looked up in my slouched down position, and I could see the trees and the streetlights. I remember thinking, 'Just look at the trees and the streetlights. Keep your car centered between the trees on both sides of the car and you will be in the middle of the street. You can drive out like that.' That's what I did, Bobby. I looked at the trees and streetlights. I kept them at equal distances to the side of my car and drove a block out of the kill zone. I never looked out of the front windshield."

I shook my hand as if I had a cramp from writing. I told Rick to stop talking. My hand wasn't cramping, I was ready to cry. He walked away, presumably to answer a text. My head was down and I was shielding my eyes with my hand. He came back and gave me the respect to wait to talk again till I looked up.

Rick pointed at the dog shit in the grass. "These nice people," and Rick pointed out several park visitors walking their dogs, "walk their dogs and let them shit in the grass then don't pick it up. I hate to step in dog shit Bobby."

So like Rick to call rude people, nice people.

"When I got to 19th and Olive Ave. I saw headlights coming at us. I thought, 'Oh, Fuck, they're coming to finish us off and kill us.' Again, I was terrified, I was defenseless. Where was everyone? Where's my back up? Of course, not much time had passed from the time I had put out a call for assistance until this time. To me though, in my state so much time had elapsed. It was like a lifetime, not just a minute or two. Then a helicopter arrived. Our helicopter. The loudspeaker came on, 'Hang on, help's coming.' The trees were waving around from the rotor wash. The helicopter guided all the other units to us. When the units arrived, they rushed to our car. I feel sorry for the guys who first got there, it was something no one should probably see."

"Rick was time normal now?"

"Yes. I don't specifically know when it happened, but things were in normal time now. One of the officers said, 'Come on Rick, let's get you to the hospital.'

"I told him, 'I can't. It hurts too much. Please get me the paramedics so they can transport me.'

"He was at the driver's door, 'No Rick, we gotta go now, before you bleed out!'

"Bobby, my knee was hurting so bad, and my foot was at a nasty angle, I begged him. 'Please get the paramedics to stabilize me before I am moved.' I was holding onto the steering wheel in a death grip.

"The officer put a finger at my jaw where it meets my lower ear. That hurt and I let go of the steering wheel to shove his hand away. That's when he grabbed me and pulled me out of the car. It was excruciating. Blinding hot unbelievable, indescribable pain. They carried me over and laid me down in the back seat of a radio car. They had rolled the rear window down and propped up my busted leg on the window. If I was in pain before, now I was in hell. Five cops plus me were in that radio car. How they fit them all in, I have no idea. The drive was agonizing. It was a million years of time and a terrible blinding haze of pain. Every second an eternity. When I got to the hospital, one of my friends looked at me. 'Rick, what the fuck?' He grabbed me under the arms and started pulling me out of the back seat. My leg was banging around. My gun got hung up on the seat belt. He couldn't get me out. I screamed, 'LET GO, YOU'RE HURTING ME MORE!' Finally, thank God, the hospital staff came and got me out and took me to the emergency room. A little later I looked over, and there was my partner lying about 20 feet away. I thought, 'Oh he's not dead.' But he was, they just hadn't covered his face. There was a nurse next to me. I was talking to her trying to get her attention. This went on for a little while. She was ignoring me. I had this scary thought, 'She can't hear me.' I thought and really believed, 'Oh shit, I'm dead.' I was panicked. 'I'm having an out of body experience. I'm dead. No one can hear me.'

"She finally responded to me. 'I'm sorry I was busy. Can I help you?'

"'Yes ma'am,' I answered, so relieved I wasn't dead like I thought I was moments ago, 'Are you going to put a catheter in me?'

"'Yes, we're going to have to.'

"Bobby, I thought I was dead and I was worried about a catheter. I was thinking I must have a baby dick, shriveled up from fright. How embarrassing, to have a baby dick. I didn't want her to see I had a baby dick."

I looked at Rick and started laughing.

"Some cops went and picked up my wife and brought her to the hospital. My head was wrapped like a mummy. When they wheeled me from the emergency room, all I saw were all the guys from the shift. It was a sea of blue. I was able to wave to them. It was hard. I mean it physically hurt a lot to wave, but I waved anyway. I didn't want them to worry about me."

I looked at Rick, "And your recovery?"

"It was long and hard. It hurt." When Rick walks, he lifts his right leg and throws his foot in front of him. "Sir, I wanted to tell you, you know the probation officer who we were going to have a beer with later that night?"

"Yeah?"

"Her name is Lynn, sir. She came on her own time and helped my wife take care of my kids. I don't even know how to thank her enough. I can't thank her enough. She is such a beautiful person. Solid. Another thing, Bobby? You know how us cops are tight? Well, I really saw the outpouring of support and love from my department and our union. The department cared about me. So many individuals came forward to help. Too many to count. They don't know how much it meant and means to me. I will never ever forget them."

Silence again between us.

"You know, Bobby, I am married to a wonderful woman who gave me three great kids. I don't think, no, I know, I don't tell her enough that I love her. My kids were young when I got shot up. She became a stabilizing force in our lives at a time when I was a mess, you know recovering from my injuries. She is strong as steel."

He got that faraway look again. "My wife, what a woman she is to put up with my fat ass… She is a cop's wife." The way he said it made me believe there was no higher station a woman could hope to attain than being a cop's wife.

*****

Rick has all these little and some not so little scars. In addition to the compression in the side of his head, he has scars and pucker marks on his right leg.

"Look at this, Bobby," he showed me one of his fingers. Part of the nail was growing in separate like he had another nail coming in on the side of his full nail. "Bobby, I can't explain it, but after the shooting, while I was in the hospital the backs of all my fingers were all chewed up. Raw and a little bloody. The only thing I can think of is when I was in the car and everything was disintegrating it was scraping the skin off of the back of my fingers. Something took off part of this finger (he held up the finger with the funny nail), and the nail never grew back normal."

*****

"After the shooting, all the cops set up a huge perimeter and went to work. They found the initial guy who had crossed the street and was eye fucking us. He had gone over a couple of blocks and climbed a tree in someone's backyard. Of course he was a gang member. When they got him to the station, he refused to talk. Bobby, the funny thing is I knew him. When he refused to talk to the other detectives, he said the only person he would talk to was me. The detectives brought in my badge and identification. It had been pulled from me in the hospital after the shooting. I used to wear it on a chain around my neck. They went back into the interview room and plopped down my identification and badge. The gang member was all hard and said, 'Who's that?' The detectives cleaned off some of the blood so my picture was showing. When the gang member saw it was me, he said, 'That was him in the car?'"

"Why you Rick? Why'd he only want to talk to you?"

"Bobby, several things sir. Can I back up the story?" Rick was talking yelling again.

"About a month before this shooting, I met one of the Sheriff's Carson gang detectives. She told me she had made this guy on a murder in Compton. It turned out it was the same guy who eye fucked us as he was crossing the street, right before I got shot. I knew him and told her I would try to find him and lock him up."

Rick paused, "I'm sorry, Bobby, let me back up again. You need to understand how it all went down. Before all that, the reason I knew him was that he had thrown a party at his house and it went sideways. There were too many people there, and it was loud and out of control. A lot of us cops, including our gang unit showed up to break it up. The cops were doing what they had to do to handle a lot of drunk, gang members, and their friends. While the cops were doing that, I was talking to this guy's mom. I was comforting her. I was telling her we had to be there, but that everything was going to be okay, just it was too loud. I told her not to worry we would be gone as soon as everyone left. She took comfort from me talking to her. I made her feel like everything was going to be okay. Bobby, because of that, as far as I could tell, the guy trusted me. I think that's why he said he would only talk to me.

"Oh Bobby, can I tell you this sir?"

I smiled, smiled at Rick's unbelievable manners. Don't you love him too?

"A nice lady who lived down the street got shot. I don't know her, but she was in her house, and one of the bullets meant for me went through her stucco wall and hit her. She called 911, but the paramedics couldn't get to her because of the streets being sealed off. She was pregnant and went into labor. Well, one of the cops was an emergency medical technician and got her first aid and got her to the hospital. She had a baby.

"Oh, and Bobby, remember those eight to ten guys hanging around the street, the initial ones got my attention?"

"Yeah."

"Bobby the reason they were there was they were going to kill a rival gang member. The other gang member lived about a block away. These guys were going to walk over to his house. The other gang member was a guy in his early thirties. He had a nine-year-old daughter who just happened to be having a sleepover with her friends that night. One of those ten gang member guys was going to knock on this guy's door. When he answered the door, they were going to kill him. Then they were all going to completely spray the house with gunfire."

I looked at Rick. For a second he had that faraway look again.

Then he looked me in the eye. "Bobby, if it hadn't been for us, thirteen or fourteen little girls would have been shot, hurt, and killed." A little quiet pause went by. "I don't like what I had to go through. But if I had to be the guinea pig, my partner and I, to save those girls, those innocent kids, it was worth it. My partner and I saved some lives that night, Bobby. I'm proud of that. The funny thing is the father heard what happened that night. He found out those guys were going to kill him and spray his house with gunfire. This thirty-year-old gang member told the detectives to thank me for saving his little girl's life. I never met the nice man."

I asked Rick, "The guy who shot you, and killed your partner, what did he get?"

"He's on death row, sir. He was sentenced to death row."

"Bobby, you know the worst part. I never got to shoot my gun. I couldn't protect myself and my partner. I never had a chance. I still don't know where the shooter was. I never saw him. That was the worst of it."

Rick had that faraway look again. It seemed to me he was looking at the sun coming through the leaves in the trees in the park. Then he said to no one in particular, "Look at all these nice people with their dogs."

*****

Rick Delfin, my friend, received the Long Beach Police Department Medal of Valor. It is the highest award his department can bestow upon its sworn officers. He also received the Purple Heart for his actions on the night of April 29, 2000.

Chapter 12

Close Calls and Common Sense

1986. I was riding a two-man car at West Hollywood Station. My partner and I had been academy classmates. I trained at Lennox where my first week we had six murders. He had trained at West Hollywood where there were maybe six murders a year. Maybe.

We got a call of a battery that just occurred. We found the victim at the pay phone booth where he called 911. It was about midnight.

He was bleeding profusely from his nose, which looked broken. His eyes were watering, and he was slobbering as he cried. I was trying to talk to him. "Sir, what happened?"

Nothing. I got nothing from him. Nothing but crying, bleeding and sputtering. Again, I asked, "Sir, what happened, who did this to you? I'd like to help you out, but I can't understand anything you're saying."

Again, more bloody sputtering and crying. This went on for about a minute. I couldn't get any information from him at all. I decided to use my superior intellect and change the subject. The tact I was using was going nowhere. "Sir, what's your name?"

Again, nothing but some blubbering. Then I asked the question. The question changed it all. I don't know why, but it did. "Sir do you have any identification?"

The blubbering stopped. Instantly. Weird. The hair went up in the back of my neck. He stared at me with that "FUCK YOU" look. "Identification?" he said, "IDENTIFICATION?!! I'LL SHOW YOU IDENTIFICATION!!!"

As quickly as a hand could move, he moved his right hand to his left breast under his jacket. My mind screamed, "GUN!" I reached up with my left hand and clamped it over his right wrist, which was under his jacket. I had an iron grip on his wrist and would not let it move. When I reached for his arm, I had simultaneously and without thinking ducked about five inches and drew my gun with my right hand and pointed it at him. My gun was by my hip pointed upwards towards his chest. I was slightly turned sideways, and my gun was out of his reach.

He said in a begging beseeching voice, "Don't kill me, please don't kill me."

I was angry, scared and very much on edge. "DON'T move your fucking hand!!!" While still pointing my gun at him I slid my left hand from his wrist and over his hand and felt through the jacket and could feel there was no gun there. "Take your hand out slowly, really slow." He did as I said. I patted him down, and he was unarmed. His identification was in his inner left jacket pocket. My partner was standing there with his thumbs hooked in his pants pocket throughout this whole incident.

"Why did you do that?" I asked the man.

He started crying and blubbering again, "I'm sorry man. I'm sorry."

After we finished handling the call, my partner said, "I should have drew-down on him."

To this day I don't understand why they did what they did. When I say that, I mean I don't understand why my partner was just standing there and why the man did what he did. What I do know is it was really close. I almost shot him.

*****

1985. I was the passenger in a two-man car. It was about four in the afternoon. We turned right from 120th Street to southbound Western Ave. There was a gas station on the southwest corner. Right behind the gas station was a little strip mall. Behind the strip mall was a huge parking lot for a K-Mart store. As we turned south on Western Ave., I caught a glimpse of a man running between the gas station and the strip mall. When I saw him, he was making the turn behind the strip mall toward the K-Mart parking lot. As he ran and made the left turn, I saw, just for a millisecond his right arm drop. Then he was behind the strip mall and out of my sight. I thought I saw a gun. It was black, and I thought it could have been a pipe, but I wasn't sure.

"Kenny, I think I just saw a guy running with a gun. He's behind the strip mall."

"Oh bullshit," Kenny said.

About a second later we had cleared the strip mall and had a clear view of the parking lot. I saw the man running through the parking lot with his right arm extended and he was pointing a gun. "KENNY, HE'S GOT A FUCKING GUN!!!"

We went into autopilot. I got my keys out to unlock the shotgun. Kenny got on the radio. People in the parking lot were ducking behind cars; cars were skidding out of the parking lot. Pandemonium.

We pulled up behind the man. We were fifteen feet behind him. He was so intent on his target, he never saw us. He had a black semi-automatic pistol in his right hand. I had the shotgun in my hands. Kenny stopped, and I kicked open the patrol car door. "FREEZE, POLICE, DON'T TURN AROUND! DROP THE GUN!"

He started turning around. "DON'T TURN AROUND!!! DON'T TURN AROUND!!! DROP THE GUN!!!"

As clearly as I'm writing this now, I can see him. I had the shotgun pointed right at his chest; he was now facing me. I had already racked a live round in the chamber, the safety was off. I could see him as I looked over the front sight of the shotgun. There was no way I could miss. The shotgun has no pull in the trigger. No forgiveness. In other words, when you pull the trigger it just fires, unlike a handgun where you pull the trigger for a while then it fires. You either fire or you don't. As he faced me his gun hand moved. I was going to pull the trigger. And now I was so calm, my decision had been made. There was no turning back. Mentally I knew I was going to shoot the man. "I got him Kenny," I said calmly, "I got him." I could feel the pressure on my fingertip, the man's gun hand was moving. This was so ugly. Every fiber of my body was concentrating on where the barrel of the gun was pointing. Even though the gun was moving, I wanted him to drop it. Things were happening slowly. His hand was moving slowly. It was just fractions of an inch until I pulled the trigger. A millisecond. And he was in control of what I was going to do. I was so calm. Then he dropped the gun.

Kenny ran to him and bounced his head off the hood of the radio car. I was now impotent; my hands were full of shotgun. Kenny handcuffed him while I covered him with the shotgun. Kenny and I knew what to do without speaking a word, knowing full well if things went sideways, Kenny would push the man away and it would be either shotgun time or baton time. Understand we had still not secured the weapon the man had dropped. After the man was handcuffed, Kenny picked the gun up from the ground and showed it to me. It was a BB gun. You couldn't tell it was a BB gun even when you first held it. You had to look at the barrel. It was black and looked just like a real gun.

The man was the gas station owner. An irate customer had thrown a trash can at him, and he chased the guy through the parking lot with the gun. We just happened to see the tail end of it.

We let the guy go.

Kenny and I went to eat right after that. I was having trouble eating. He looked at me and said, "I'm glad we didn't kill that guy."

If we had, the media would have described how two Los Angeles County Deputy Sheriff's had killed a poor gas station owner just because he had a BB gun.

It's scary how many close calls happen every day. They happen all the time, every day. I could tell you so many more I've had. Suffice it to say I am glad I only shot or shot at those who really deserved it… but in the scenarios described above, in my mind at the time the incidents were unfolding I was justified in using deadly force. Whether or not those in judgment of my actions would have agreed is another subject.

*****

I've been in court and heard prosecuting attorneys and judges say when people beat the hell out of robbers, "Why didn't they call the cops?"

Around 1983 a friend of mine who lived in Venice, California came home one day. He was a World War II veteran, and at this time he was nearing sixty years old. You need to understand this Englishman had seen hand-to-hand combat against the Germans and had survived. Even though at the time he was close to sixty, he was unbelievably hard as nails. When he opened the door to his house, his door opened but bumped something and sort of bounced back toward him. His wife was right behind him. He immediately shoved the door hard and pinned a man who was behind the door against the wall. In an instant, he cleared the door and was face to face with a man he didn't know. "Don't move."

The man moved.

My friend pinned him against the wall; his wife was screaming. Again, my friend said, "DON'T MOVE!!!"

The man shoved hard against my friend who was a wall of steel. That was it. My friend literally beat the stranger, half to death, until he didn't move anymore. L.A.P.D. arrived about five minutes later. It was a pretty good response time, but they were still too late. The incident was over. They proceeded to berate my friend for beating the man. "Why did you beat him? You didn't need to beat him so badly," and on and on. It went so far he heard them talking about arresting him. They were actually discussing it.

Sad. Someone comes into your house, and you get in trouble. He had no idea if the man was armed. He had no idea if there was another suspect with him who also might attack him. In my mind, all bets are off. He didn't kill the man; he just made sure he was no longer a threat. I say good job. I say commendable restraint for not killing him. I guess he should have just called the cops and waited while the guy pulled a gun on him?

Furthermore, I suppose as I write this there will be some who will use this book as a, "See we need to enact stricter gun laws!" But there are times, like the scenario mentioned above, when help will not be able to make it in time. There are times in people's lives where they face death, and the result is black and white: they either live, or they die.

In the true scenarios presented in this book, most of the incidents occurred before any help could arrive. These were cops and "they" couldn't get help, their partners, there before the incident was over. Sure we would have welcomed the help, but these things for the most part happen in seconds. If these events occur this quickly, law enforcement, in most instances will not be able to get there in time to help.

How about this? You are getting into your car, and someone comes and puts a gun to you and tells you they are taking your car. Your baby is in the backseat. What do you do?

I know what I'd do.

Let's say someone sees this criminal pulling a gun on you as soon as it happens and calls 911. Dispatch answers the phone and gets the location, finds out what is happening and puts out the call. By now thirty seconds has gone by. The incident is now over. You've already been either shot, or your kid is being driven away by a stranger. Or even worse, both. Even if a cop just happens to be on the next block, it will take him another minute to get to you. Too late. Call the cops? There goes that theory. As much as we want to, and believe me we want to, "WE CAN'T SAVE YOU!!!" The truth is there are bad people out there who prey on good people.

Furthermore, the cities that have the strictest gun laws, Detroit, Chicago, Washington, D.C and New Orleans have the highest crime in the United States. Shame on you newscasters, legislators, politicians and lawmakers who think people should only have so many bullets or certain guns. You cannot be so ignorant that you actually believe outlawing guns and bullets will stop crime. It is a fact criminals still obtain firearms no matter what the law is. Criminals don't care about laws. They ignore them. Outlawing guns and bullets will not make you any safer. It just makes law-abiding citizens impotent because they follow the laws and no longer can protect themselves.

Around 1998 my parents, who at the time were in their seventies, were home. It was midday. All of a sudden, the dog started barking at the door. My mother who is severely disabled from a horrific car accident went to the front door. There was a man there. My mother shooed the dog away, and suddenly the man was opening the screen door. She immediately slammed the front door closed. My parents kept a pole wedged under the doorknob by the front door. The man was slamming into the door trying to break it down. While this was going on, she was screaming for my father as she put the wedge under the front doorknob. All of a sudden, the door frame broke open, and the threshold and door began caving in. The man was partially inside the house. He was reaching through the broken doorframe into the house trying to grab my mother. She had her full body weight against the door and doorframe holding it up, keeping the man outside. Every time he reached for her she kept moving to the side. Finally, the man got his arm, upper body and head into the house. He looked up and was staring down the barrel of a gun, which was in my father's hands. Unbeknownst to my mother, my father had got a gun and was behind her aiming at the man. When the man saw the gun, he stopped, pulled himself out of the door and ran.

What if you absolutely need to shoot someone to save yourself or your family? In some of the stories here the suspects were shot many times and were still a threat. How many bullets are enough? Five? Ten? Fifteen? Remember you're talking to a guy who started patrol with a six-shooter and two reloads. That's eighteen bullets. NOT ENOUGH! I need more bullets to protect myself. And believe me, and I sincerely hope it never happens to you, but if you need to protect yourself, you will need more bullets too.

If you cannot handle a car because you are such a bad driver, and you think you might kill someone, then you shouldn't drive. Or if you believe you will cut off your hand by using a power saw then don't use one. You should not ever operate any machine you cannot handle. A gun is a machine. Nothing more, nothing less. And just like any other machine or tool, it can hurt you if you do not use it properly. A carpenter carries a hammer on his belt, and no one looks twice because the purpose of that tool is not to harm anyone. However, I've seen people who were hit in the head with a hammer. It's very nasty. A gun by itself cannot harm anyone. It is the intent of the person using that tool or machine which causes the damage. The intent of the person does not change whether the hammer, the car, the saw, or the gun is outlawed or not. A person will do good or bad based on their inherent beliefs, not what gun laws dictate. Now some of you are entirely opposed to having a gun. That's perfectly okay; you should not have one, but don't lie to me and tell me I will be safer if we outlaw guns. Don't trample on my 2nd Amendment constitutional right to bear arms, or my God given right to protect myself. I took an oath to protect the constitution against all enemies foreign and "domestic." My oath did not mention protecting a Mayor, a Governor, a Senator, a Congressman or the President of the United States. It was to defend the Constitution. Who is the enemy here? Who is committing treason by trying to change the Constitution? Me? Throughout my career, I did my best protect as many people as I could and to put as many criminals in jail as possible. It's a pretty common theme throughout this book. I did all of this only to see criminals who should be executed or locked up for life let go. Only to see them hurt innocents time and again.

To you district attorneys, we did not join to be peace officers to be spit upon, hit, kicked, knifed or shot. We joined to help people. I often hear of district attorney's flippant attitude that getting hit, or spit upon or even shot is part of an officer's job. Yes, sometimes it happens. But to have to fight to get an "assault with a deadly weapon" charge, or "attempted murder on a peace officer" charge filed because you feel it's "part" of their job is ridiculous. Additionally, our own departments discourage officers from arresting people for assault on a peace officer if someone spits on them, lest an officer be perceived as sparking too many violent confrontations. Let me tell you folks, when you are dealing with drunks, dope addicts, jealous out of control husbands, wives, or boyfriends or girlfriends, gang members or just plain wacko people every day all day long, guess what? When you are physically putting your hands-on people, it's going to happen. You are going to get assaulted. One of my academy classmates was in three shootings in his first 18 months of being on patrol. They were all good shootings, trust me. That is, one shooting every six months. So, what's going on here? Where is the understanding by the courts or the citizens of the extreme violence our peace officers encounter? We are not nurses or teachers; we deal with some very bad people.

When I was a detective, we had a filing district attorney (a filing deputy district attorney reviews cases brought to them by detectives and decides whether to charge the suspect or not). He told me when he was a new deputy district attorney, he worked under Evelle Younger. He said Mr. Younger's approach was to file a case if you thought the person was guilty and if there was any chance of winning in court. The attitude was, "We may lose some, but we'll win a whole lot more." This deputy district attorney then said his way of looking at things had changed. Nowadays cases are only filed if you are positive you can win them. Why? Two reasons. One is that cases clog up the courts. The more cases filed, the more slowly the court works. The second reason is "elections." District Attorneys are politicians. They want to get reelected. The higher the conviction rate, the better the chances of a deputy district attorney being reelected. Elections should have no place in trying to protect society.

A judge can hold a citizen and charge him with "contempt of court." Who has shown contempt for our citizens? For its peace officers? Our own system beats the officers down. Our own system lets these very violent criminals out and lets the citizens and society down also. Attempted murder felons should not be out of prison in four, five, six, or seven years. Who is contemptuous here? I think you citizens can see this point from the firsthand experiences of the storytellers throughout this book. Did you notice I did not say attempted murder on peace officer felons? You see I believe all life is precious and sacred. The life of a peace officer is no more or less valuable than a non-peace officer. That ladies and gentlemen is why we joined, to protect life. That is why we are special. Because we, peace officers, lay it on the line.

One word to you badge-heavy, or rude officers. Yes, you heard it here first. I admit there are some who abuse their power. Shame on you. That badge does not give you any special privileges. The damage you do to the officers who try every day to do the right thing is incalculable. Get your act together.

*****

West Hollywood, circa 1989. A man was walking around in the hot summer night. It was around 10:30 at night. People without air conditioning had their doors open with their screen doors closed. The man entered an apartment courtyard and saw a woman sitting in her living room watching television. Her husband was asleep in a recliner. He opened the screen door and hit her on the head, severely stunning her. He removed her nightgown and sodomized her. The husband woke up, and the man beat him, caving in his head. He then went back and finished sodomizing the woman. When he was finished, he killed her.

What a way to end a marriage. The couple was in their eighties. The young man was in his late twenties, about five foot ten and about two hundred and fifty pounds. All muscle, all savage madness, someone who should have been locked up or executed years before. I think about this event at times and go to a deep place in my soul. The eighty-year-old man had no chance in hand to hand confrontation with that animal. What if he could have gotten to a gun?

Chapter 13

Thank You

Wyatt Earp. What do you think? I'll tell you what I think. Setting aside the reasons that brought the shooters to the O.K. Corral, these were men who were desperately fighting for their lives. And depending on where you were standing on that day, you saw and perceived things differently. There is testimony that shows neither the shooters nor the witnesses knew who shot first. It started that fast. I can guarantee you one thing. Time slowed down for those involved. GUARANTEED! It was a lifetime to the shooters. And although so many movies have been made about it, the stories you have read in this book will give you a better picture of what it was really like, better than any movie you've seen. The shooting at the O.K. Corral was fast and desperate to outside observers. With so many people shooting it still lasted no more than 30 seconds. To the observers, it was a quick thing, with multiple people quickly shooting, hitting but mostly missing each other. Missing each other from six to ten feet away. But it was a lifetime to those involved.

Wyatt's testimony at his hearing after the event is preserved in writing. It's on the Internet. Do a search of "Wyatt Earp's testimony." In his written statement he tells of going to meet the Clantons and McLowrys to disarm them. He speaks it was his duty to do so. He tells of Sheriff Behan telling him and Doc Holiday and his brothers not to go. He said they would be killed. Then Sheriff Behan changes his story. He tells them he disarmed the clan. What Wyatt said was he put his gun, which was in his hand, into his pocket. What's going on here? It's confusing, and I am sure Wyatt and his group were confused also. It's like that going into a gunfight. One thing is for sure, Behan and Wyatt are on opposite sides of the fence. Behan, the Sheriff, walks away from the group, away from the O.K. Corral. Who knows what Wyatt was thinking at this point? He tells that after the shooting starts, he does not shoot at Ike Clanton, the instigator of the event. A man who had conspired to kill Wyatt, and his brothers. Earp admitted he felt he had every right to kill Ike Clanton for the threats he had made. After Wyatt shot four times at perceived threats, Ike ran to Wyatt and told him he was not armed. Wyatt, in the midst of the gunfight, shook him off and told him to run away. That is not the voice of a cold-blooded killer, but the voice of a lawman. He could not kill him because his duty would not allow him to. He shot those who he perceived to be an immediate threat to him. Ike Clanton, who he most likely hated, was not an immediate threat. Again, my respect for yet another lawman, like the ones in this book, deepens.

Let me tell you some more truths. I have three cousins. Two are Los Angeles County Deputy Sheriffs. One is a Los Angeles Police Officer. Four of us in total. Two of us have been shot. You read those stories here. Another cousin had someone try to take his gun away, and he shot the attacker to prevent himself from being killed. The last cousin had an incident where he was wrestling on the ground with a suspect, while getting shot at by a second suspect and his partners were simultaneously shooting the guy shooting at him. That's all four of us. Four for four, who have either been shot, shot at, or has had to kill someone to prevent himself from being shot. No glamorized movie, or a snippet in a newspaper. These are real-life events, tough men and women, desperately fighting to live while still doing what is right.

Heroes? A few chapters back I asked you if you could identify what a hero was. Well, let me tell you what I think. Wyatt Earp was brave, but no braver than the men and women out in the streets in the present day. Wyatt Earp was a hero. Why? After the O.K. Corral, numerous events far too complicated to recount in this book took place. Let us say Wyatt went after those who were responsible for breaking the law. Those who Sheriff Behan protected. He went out after knowing what could happen to him. He went out after one of his brothers was ambushed and shot. He went out after one of his brothers was shot in the back and killed. He went out after those men, knowing he could be killed. I like the Wyatt Earp story. I think if I had met him I would have liked him. But I don't idolize him. Why not? Idolize is the wrong word. I view him as a comrade. Someone who tried to do the right thing even if it might cost him his life. The real heroes are the people like the people in this book. Why? Because after going through what they went through, they went back out. They went back out in the streets. They went out knowing full well what could happen to them. They looked death right in the face and literally laughed at it. They chose to possibly face it again. That's a hero. Society idolizes "sports athletes," "actors," "celebrities," as heroes. I don't. I appreciate their talent, but I do not idolize them. They are not heroes to me. My background check to be a peace officer was more extensive, more difficult than to become the president of the United States. I had to provide proof of being a United States citizen. I never used any drugs, including marijuana. I had perfect credit and have always paid my bills. I had a perfect work record, perfect. I almost was disqualified for having three speeding tickets within five years. That was it, the full extent of my bad life. Three speeding tickets. I don't idolize people who are drug users. And I don't excuse the bad behavior we see in the sports, entertainment or the political world just because someone is famous. When were they, heroes? When have they faced death and then gone forth to face it again?

Every night the officers are out there, slowly driving around in the middle of the night. Windows down in freezing weather, listening for sounds that are not normal, sniffing the air to find dangerous people. Stopping gang members, drug addicts, so we can all be safe, all the while knowing they could die.

No disrespect to you nice people out there... but where are you in the middle of the night?

*****

Years ago, circa 1987, my partner and I would drive through Plummer

Park in West Hollywood in our radio cars. We'd wave at the moms and kids. One sunny Sunday morning we were driving through the park and stopped by the tennis court. There were benches there, and an old man was sitting. He must have been in his mid-seventies, but he looked very fit. He sat in the sun with his tennis racket, peacefully waiting for his tennis court to become available. We were probably ten feet away from him. He smiled at us, and we smiled back and nodded our heads in acknowledgment of his hello.

He slowly got up and walked to our open driver's door window. "How'ya doin?"

"Pretty good," we answered.

"20 years L.A.P.D.," he said identifying himself with obvious pride.

"Oh cool," we answered.

We chit chatted for a little bit. Nothing important, really. Just stuff, the weather, a little about where he had worked, how his tennis game was going. Just a couple of minutes of small talk.

As we said our goodbyes, he said, "God bless you guys," and he patted my arm very warmly.

I was puzzled as to why he said what he said, his parting words to us so heartfelt. I didn't know how to respond. I was at a loss, so I simply said, "Thank you."

He understood something then I didn't, but I now do.

I would like to personally say to all of you out there in those cars, in uniform, a walking, living, breathing target; to those of you who stop to say hello to the kids, who drive down the streets and make the old people feel better, safer; who give up your weekends and nights with your families, birthdays and holidays with your loved ones; to those of you who place yourselves in harm's way to stop the two-legged animals, the predators of those weaker than themselves, hunting the devil most people pretend doesn't exist; to those of you who are frustrated at every turn by the injustices imposed by the criminal court system that continually let those free who have proved themselves to be habitual dangerous criminals; to those of you whose love for your fellow man is greater than the love you have for yourself, I would like to say, "God Bless you."

To My Fellow Red Dot Members:

These pages leave so much unsaid.

The author has purposely left out the physical healing of those involved in these stories. The author has purposely left out the psychological aspects, effects that these near-death experiences have had on the storytellers. This is our business, and not for those who don't understand. I don't know if you can understand unless you have actually faced and accepted you are going to die.

Suffice it to say we are damaged. But then isn't everyone to some extent? Some more than others... but everyone interviewed, all the storytellers, have been and still are working, productive, contributors to society in some fashion. It's not in our blood to quit. Oh, we walk with limps. Our bullets still hurt. Even years later. We can't sleep at night, sometimes from physical pain, sometimes from nightmares. Oh yes, this is so true. We keep it hidden; it is never far from the surface. But we still get up every day, most times early in the morning and go to work.

The information missing in this account was purposely left out, out of respect and in deference to the members of the Red Dot Club, you storytellers. You storytellers who were, and are so brave to bare your soul, no different than if you were standing naked in front of the world, to tell it like it really is. To you members of the Red Dot Club, you have my eternal, and utmost profound respect and gratitude.

Your friend and fellow Red Dot Club Member,

Robert Rangel

In Appreciation

I would like to thank those who without their help this book would not have been possible.

First and foremost, I would like to thank my parents, Robert and Marie. You have read countless revisions of this manuscript, crying each time, but still, you carried on. When I had headaches, and couldn't sleep at night as a result of these stories you encouraged me to keep going.

To my sister Christy Lifosjoe, I would like to say thank you for all your patience in my indecisiveness with the book cover. This illustration is an true reflection of your artistic talents.

And... last but certainly not least. To my talented editor Fred Bobola. You poured your heart and soul out to help me get this project out on schedule. You too my friend had many sleepless nights as these stories horrified and touched your soul. But you persevered. I am indebted to you. You took a morass of words and made it into a book I am proud to show the world. It's as if you bought a rusted Volkswagen Beetle from the junkyard, and made it into a Rolls Royce. Thank you.

To my daughter-in-law, Jessica, thank you for refining this book for the second edition.

Check out my website at robertrangelbooks.com

Afterword

Since the release of the first edition of this book, I have had a lot of feedback from many readers. Many have been cops.

Wow!!! Your comments have been amazing.

I cannot share them all, but I will close in the same vein as I started:

To Jim Mahone,

Many who had you as their drill instructor have now read this book and have personally told me that they, as I, have also credited you with saving their lives, and the lives of citizens they no longer know. You know not the good you have done.

Collectively I would again like to say thank you.

You taught us many things, but you failed in one aspect.

You see, Jim, you told us to not take it personally. You told us we would see horrific things and experience many injustices. You told us we would not be able to fix them. You told us to not take it personally. You were so right.

To have the ability to not care makes for a long career…but, we joined because we do care. Therein lays the contradiction.

You see you never taught us how not to care. Or how to deal with those horrific things. Those injustices. We have had careers of our own now.

How can one not be affected by it all, for it to not make a difference? I've asked, and no one has been able to give me "that" answer.

So my friend I take comfort in knowing you did your best for us and taught us all you knew. I leave the unanswerable question to a higher power, to God.

If I ever get that answer, I will share it… actually, upon reflection, I don't think I will.

About the Author

Robert is a native of Los Angeles. He had his own business at eighteen. Seeking adventure, and a strong desire to help his fellow man, he sold his business at twenty-five and joined the Los Angeles Sheriff's Department. Thirteen years later, after numerous on-duty injuries (mostly bullets), he medically retired as a detective. He then traveled the world protecting princes and princesses originating from three different countries. The Royals stopped traveling, and Robert found himself in a new career outside of banks with the sole purpose of stopping armed bank robberies (more bullets). He is currently a civilian investigator for a major police department conducting pre-hire peace officer background investigations (not so many bullets). Married twice, he is now womanless but has three sons. He still resides in Los Angeles but loves the forest. He'd like you to buy a couple of his books so he can move there… watch, with his luck you'll buy the books, he'll move to the forest and get shot by a hunter (stray bullets).

Made in the USA
San Bernardino, CA
24 March 2019